Mentioning the War

Essays & Reviews 1999-2011

Kevin Higgins

salmonpoetry

Published in 2012 by
Salmon Poetry
Cliffs of Moher, County Clare, Ireland
Website: www.salmonpoetry.com
Email: info@salmonpoetry.com

ISBN 978-1-908836-12-0

COVER ARTWORK: © *Lisavan* | *Dreamstime.com*
COVER DESIGN: *Siobhán Hutson*

Salmon Poetry receives financial support from
The Arts Council / An Chomhairle Ealaíon

For Mary Higgins

(April 25th, 1942 – May 31st, 2011)

Acknowledgements

Acknowledgements are due to the editors of the following publications in which these essays and reviews first appeared:

Vallum (Montreal, Canada); *Books In Canada: The Canadian Review of Books*; *Red Banner*; *The Galway Advertiser*; *Canadian Notes & Queries*; *Poetry Ireland Newsletter*; *ACTWRITE* The magazine of the ACT Writers Centre (Canberra, Australia); *muc mhór dhubh*; *Nthposition.com*; *Criterion*; *The Journal* (UK); *The Journal of the Galway Archaeological and Historical Society*; *The Wolf* (UK); *Poetry—Reading it, Writing it, Publishing it* (Ed. Jessie Lendennie, Salmon Poetry, 2009); *The Watchful Heart—A New Generation of Irish Poets* (Ed. Joan McBreen, Salmon Poetry, 2009)

'Back Home To Ireland' was broadcast on RTE Radio One's *Sunday Miscellany*.

'The Poetry Reading Escapes From The Victorian Drawing Room' was presented as a paper at the First Galway Conference of Irish Studies—*Orality and Modern Irish Culture*—hosted by the Centre for Irish Studies, NUI Galway 7-10 June, 2006

'The Condemned Apple', originally published on *Nthposition.com*, was also published in Albanian translation in the Albanian newspapers *Ndryshe* and *Shekulli*.

A number of the essays also appeared in the pamphlet *Poetry, Politics & Dorothy Gone Horribly Astray* (Lapwing Press, 2006).

Contents

Foreword by Darrell Kavanagh

It is easy to be right for the wrong reasons—all that is necessary is a bit of luck. In fact, not even luck is required—you just need to keep repeating the same thing for long enough, and eventually, for at least a while, your dogma will reflect reality. Even those cults who predict the end of the world with such great certainty will be proved correct, eventually.

It is also possible to be sometimes wrong, but for the right reasons, although this is much more difficult, as it requires independent thought. The late, great, Christopher Hitchens proved that. He identified the rise of fundamentalism (whether of the religious or political flavours) as a "clear and present danger", threatening the achievements of the Enlightenment, and so chose that as his battleground. In doing so, he made himself unpopular in so-called "progressive" circles, not so much because of his support for this, or that, war, as his glee in slaughtering sacred cows. It was all very well when he applied his polemical talents against Henry Kissinger, but when the same principles were deployed against Bill Clinton and various even less justifiable fetishes of the left, people started screaming "traitor!". What those people will never realize is that their simplistic dogmas leave an honest free-thinker no choice.

Which brings us to the current collection, *Mentioning the War*, a selection of Kevin Higgins' reviews and essays over the course of the last decade or so. It is a fascinating read, which amongst other things, charts the author's path away from the "actually existing" far left, to a place where pragmatism and the least-worst option are watchwords, and uncertainty often reigns. In fact it was, I think, the absolute certainty and stubborn dogmatism of the left, in the face of a world, which despite suffering horrendous inequalities and exploitation, never looked like listening, that set Kevin off on this journey.

But the story is not half as dry or depressing as I might have just made it sound. The humanity of Kevin's writing, together with his provocative imagery, (which those familiar with his poetry will know all about), make sure of that. He obviously enjoys the freedom from having to toe a party line, and ironically, his conclusions on the social role of literature and art end up having far more in common with the nuanced analysis of Marx, Trotsky, et al, than do those of their self-proclaimed modern-day disciples. And Kevin avoids all three of the sad ends to which ex-revolutionaries can come: religion, post-modernism or rabid neo-liberalism. One can understand why this often happens—there is an understandable temptation, not to say a psychological need, for the old big idea to be replaced with a new big idea. Kevin avoids this trap, despite, as you will read, a brush with American neo-conservatism along the way. In fact, he ends up dismissing the neo-con movement for precisely this reason.

So, there is inconsistency here, sometimes flat contradiction. But in the spirit of freedom of speech, Kevin's greatest preoccupation in his profession as a writer and teacher, he lets it stand. This is refreshing honesty, in a world where self-justification and excuses have become the depressing norm. Perhaps there are no answers, or at least none which we have discovered yet, and Kevin refuses the temptation to invent them. This is a service to all of us who are interested in truth. Politics has for too long had to suffer simplistic "solutions" put forward by the unthinking and ignorant on all sides, in much the same way as science has to contend with the arrogant religious heckle "See! God did it", every time a difficult question, to which there is no immediate answer, arises. Sometimes the most valuable contribution to a debate is the one which admits "I don't know", because that is the spur which drives us on to study the question more deeply.

As one of his poems tells us, Kevin was taught by his father to use words as weapons, and there are plenty of delicious examples of that art here. Happily, Kevin has never been known to suffer fools or charlatans graciously. But the pieces included here where he talks about his work on the geriatric ward at the hospital; and his approach to encouraging his students, and those who attend the "Over The Edge" literary events, to find their voices, show another side of Kevin, and demonstrate a genuine empathy with his fellow primates and their struggles.

I should say a few words about the more personal material contained within this collection. There are a couple of childhood memoirs here, the first about moving back to Ireland from Britain, in the 1970s; the second about his mother's first battle with serious illness. These are deeply affecting pieces, which I shall leave the reader to consider.

Mentioning the War is an antidote to the know-nothing, don't-want-to-know-anything attitude which perverts human society. You know the sort of thing: super confident twenty-somethings, working in marketing or some other non-job, without an ounce of culture or humility, blathering about how they are their own "brand". They seem to revel in the fact that there is no longer any such thing as society (although they don't quite put it like that, and if you asked them, they would have no idea where the phase came from). One is left with a dark desire that one day they find themselves on skid row, and have their words shoved down their throats. I sometimes think we have already gone to hell, but for as long as people like Kevin still have lead in their pencils, there is hope.

Darrell Kavanagh,
Portsmouth, January 2012

INTRODUCTION BY JOHN GOODBY

For those of us who belonged in the 1970s and 1980s to the Militant Tendency, or, to give it its full name, the Revolutionary Socialist League, the experience was often formative. Until I read Kevin Higgins's work, some years back, I thought I was the only person who had tried to turn it into poetry, so discovering his was an immediate blast—a bond, and a source of envy at the subtlety and humour with which he'd pulled it off. Blending politics and his formative years in Galway and London, he'd woven the lingering love-hate relationship so many of its survivors have with the Tendency's laudable, but distorted utopian vision into the usual business of school, family rebellion and personal relationships. Because that is how it was; there was, for sure, plenty that was cultish about Militant, and it had its fair share of the social misfits and the bared-teeth zealots you find in any left-wing political organization, but it could also have the generosity of spirit that comes from having a utopian aim. In *The Boy With No Face* and *Time Gentleman, Please* (buy them, if you don't have copies already), Kevin showed that poetry could be made out of all that, however unpromising Fighting Fund appeals, interminable meetings on Perspectives or Plekhanov, placard-waving and weekly paper sales might appear as raw material. He was, I could see, a poet in the line of Gerry Murphy, Michael O'Loughlin and Thomas McCarthy, all of them among my favourites.

When I got to meet Kevin, about four years ago, it was clear that the energy he had once channelled into Militant had been used to bring about a revolution in the world of poetry in the west of Ireland. Together with his partner, the poet Susan Millar DuMars, he'd founded the now semi-legendary Over the Edge readings in Galway City Library back in 2003, and spun out of them countless other initiatives—poetry festivals, workshops, competitions, courses, slams and jams, happenings, journals. For him, poetry was a popular art; as he says at one point in *Mentioning the War*, 'Since I turned forty I have less tolerance for many things, and none at all for the idea that it's impossible to get decent turnouts at poetry readings', and the crowd at the reading I was one of the readers at proved it. There was something indefatigable about it all, and my head spun with the thought of everything he'd set in motion, and yet it was shot through with a characteristic dry humour as well, and a disarming refusal to take himself too seriously. I knew he must have tirelessly lobbied arts officials, funders, providers, sponsors and politicians, filled out endless forms and surveys, to get the funding and support for what is, by any measure, one of the brightest spots in the Irish poetry firmament. This book tells us something about the oh-so-necessary activity of the poetry-enabler, the kind of work too many poets aren't prepared to dirty their hands with. As well as a few fascinating personal pieces that tell us something about how the poet ticks, it also gives us a glimpse into the life of a poetry activist (or poetry 'cadre', to use the jargon of Militant), one who has opened up the too-reverential world of poetry for so many.

But Kevin wouldn't, I think, want anyone to buy and read his book if what was in it wasn't worth reading as writing pure and simple, as words on the page that will move, stimulate, engage and, probably not infrequently, provoke. He has a respect for the power of the word which is no respecter of persons or reputations, and that's as it should be. This second collection of his prose includes pieces written for, among others, *The Galway Advertiser* and *nthposition*, *Wolf*, *Vallum*, and *Red Banner* magazines, and *Poetry Ireland Newsletter*, showing the range of his outlets and suggesting the variety of his work. They range from short reviews and mini-essays to an interview, and can switch from superpower politics to an account of his mother's overcoming of Hodgkins' Disease—the latter all the more moving because it eschews heartstring-tugging, and is framed in the near-oblivious perspective of his childhood self. There's an arresting phrase, a new angle on a writer or a political position you thought you already knew about, in just about every piece here. Take, for example—I pick it out almost at random—the review of Martin Amis's *Koba the Dread*, 'Everything the Party Did, Said and Thought', with its notion that this account of Stalin is 'a continuation of … Amis's attempt to work out his relationship with his father Kingsley'. That precisely skewers, for me, one of the things about Amis's work which makes it so empty—the sense I get, whether it's about the Bomb or the holocaust, of an essential belatedness and opportunism, for all the verbal pyrotechnics. The insights range from the literary to the existential to the seriously amusing; from an aside on 'the awful motorway stopover that is one's own middle age' to 'A key question for any writer is what to do with his or her disgust'.

One of the things *Mentioning the War* offers, almost incidentally, is an insider's account of how to learn to write, and what Kevin Higgins has learned from the labour it took to get where he is. This paragraph, for example, needs to be appended to every Creative Writing prospectus: 'It is far better to be plagued with nerves than plagued with ego. Nerves you'll learn to control. ... The first time I read my work in public, at the Poets' Podium in Tralee in March 1997, I was suitably terrified. But if you're a beginner poet, an overdose of ego will be the end of you. It will make you see constructive criticism as personal slight. Others will listen to the available advice, improve their poems and move on ahead of you. And of course every success of theirs will hit you like a smack in the gob. They'll win the Patrick Kavanagh Award, the Hennessy, the Nobel. They'll be published by Faber and invited to read in Athens and Tokyo. You'll either give up. Or worse than that, you'll vanish down dark alleys and into whiskey bottles, consoling yourself with the fact that Kavanagh too was misunderstood in his day. I exaggerate, ever so slightly.'

And, of course, in there with the personal and the poetic is the political. The uncompromising way this comes across is what distinguishes Kevin's work from anyone else's. Politics can be amusing, of course: I recall staying with a girlfriend in Rathmines, way back, I think it was in 1984, and her taking me along to a Dublin South-East Labour Party meeting. There was an industrial dispute going on, perhaps over PAYE (Pay All You Earn), and Ruairí Quinn was on his feet berating the irresponsibility of the strikers, and the power workers in particular. Suddenly, with exquisite timing, there was a power cut and the pontificating T.D., like the rest of us, was plunged into darkness. It was as though someone had put a blanket on the parrot's cage. The mediocrity of this particular 'podgy social democrat' is caught perfectly in Kevin's review of his autobiography which ends, tellingly, with this: 'The more 'successful' Labour leaders, such as Dick Spring, Tony Blair and (perhaps) Pat Rabbitte, are usually part con-man, part believer in their own propaganda. Ruairí Quinn's ultimate weakness was that, when it came to it, even he couldn't believe a word he said. As a political charlatan, he was just a little too obvious for his own good.' And yet the Ruairí Quinns of this world, laughable and even contemptible as they are in their own way, shrink into insignificance besides the real monsters of modern history. One of the recurring themes of this book is the way that certain sections of the left still seem incapable of acknowledging this.

For Kevin, in this area, poetry and politics are one and the same thing, indivisible. 'Culture' as he points out, 'isn't a peripheral thing: it is central.' Maybe with its new President there will be at least one politician in Ireland in the future who understands this. 'Give us bread, but give us roses', ran the refrain of an old socialist song written at the turn of the last century, and it is as true today as it ever was—more so, in fact, given the atomisation of traditional working-class culture. But for most, and for the philistine sections of the left in particular it would seem, an ineradicably totalitarian turn of mind will dominate; even the best, Kevin tells us, may 'talk Trotsky—"no party line when it come to art", and all that—but act Stalin when dealing with poetry which doesn't appear to serve the cause'. We've all met these people, and perhaps felt they were a joke; but Kevin is deadly serious, and in most cases rightly. The reason why bad cultural politics is important, he insists, is 'because it gives us a taste of the type of regime the organised far left would impose were it to come to power.' These are the people who judge poetry by its content, not by anything remotely approaching aesthetic criteria. In this regard, Higgins is impeccably Marxist: both Marx and Engels themselves were *laissez-faire* when it came to the imagination, famously preferring the old royalist Balzac to the modish radical Eugène Sue. The founders of Marxism were saturated in Sophocles, Shakespeare, Cervantes, Dante and Goethe—all reactionaries in any strict political sense—but valued them for the deeper truths about society, the self and language that only artists can frame. It's in a similar spirit that Kevin praises Meaghan Delahunt's *In The Blue House*, a novel about the final year of Trotsky's life, and his affair with Frida Kahlo, because it doesn't simplify: 'how different this is', as he puts it, 'from the caricature 'Strelnikov' in *Doctor Zhivago* with his deadpan declaration about the personal life now being "dead in Russia"'. It's good to hear someone actually say that Pasternak, oppressed by Stalinism himself, of course, wasn't all perfect. Most of the time, however, it is the culturally crude and robotic ultra-left that Kevin attacks, precisely because he knows something about them from the inside; indeed, for him it is a moral obligation. 'Refusing to stay quiet about flagrant hypocrisy on the left certainly has nothing at all to do with "rejecting revolutionary socialism", but 'if there is to be any hope at all of a better and workable and democratic version of socialism, then the far left needs to undergo a complete reformation, and to this end its nose has to be rubbed in all its worst mistakes.'

There are any number of ghastly errors, of course, and various forms of Stalinism still linger on, stomping around with their graveclothes hanging off them in tatters, like the undead. Easy to laugh, these days; and yet Stalinism wrapped itself in the authority of the first socialist revolution, of which it was the perverted outcome, and used it to cover any amount of lying, bullying, spirit-crushing, fingernail-pulling persecution and mass murder, in its pursuit of power. As Kevin puts it in one of the most striking reviews collected here, of George Orwell's *Homage to Catalonia*, 'The CP leadership would rather Franco win than have a successful revolution in Spain which they did not control', and to that end they mercilessly sabotaged the Spanish revolution. Orwell kept faith with the Barcelona of the Anarchists he had witnessed before the NKVD got to work, and suffered ostracism and threats for years afterwards as a result, after just about escaping Spain with his life. But his visceral loathing of Stalinism led to him drawing up a list of names of friends who were CP members and fellow-travellers for M15 at the height of the Cold War, and here one's sympathies waver; the moral, probably, is that your enemy's enemy is rarely your friend, and that believing it's necessary to choose the least worst of two evils can involve you in repugnant behaviour. Kevin is rightly scathing about the hypocrisy of those who glossed over the massacres carried out by the Janjaweed militias at the height of the 'war on terror' because condemning Muslim Sudan was seen as abetting the Bush administration. All of which against-the-grain awkward truth-telling comes instinctively to an ex-Trotskyist, defined as Trotsky himself was (and as we all were in Militant) by opposition to Stalinism. The danger of this purity, of course, was that of negative definition; if you gaze into the abyss for too long, as Nietzsche said, it starts gazing back at you. Trotskyism, in certain crucial respects, failed because it became an inverted, mirror image of the forces that assassinated its leader and were ostensibly its mortal enemy.

Some of that whiff of the abyss may enter Kevin's own keenness to indict undoubtedly detestable attitudes; the ultra-left nose 'has to be rubbed in all its worst mistakes', after all, although to atone for your own former close proximity to those mistakes can make for a static that jams the clearer signals. Thus, while it's fair enough that 'the erosion of civil liberties which has occurred in the US since 9/11 is nothing compared to what the far Left would do were it ever again to stumble into power', and 'Fianna Fáil, Fine Gael and the Labour Party are infinitely more democratic organisations than any of those on the organised far left. They can tolerate internal dissent in a way that the far left cannot, and that is a great strength', this is only a partial truth. Western liberal capitalism has the resources to co-opt dissent, but its rawer forms, over the past decades, in Indonesia, or South Africa, or Chile, haven't, and the response of their equivalents of Fianna Fáil and Fine Gael, at least, was (to put it mildly) rather different. As for the arts, we need someone to tell us as eloquently as Kevin does of the fate of Visar Zhiti, a young Albanian poet who spent a dozen years in labour camps for some inoffensive verses in his collection *The Condemned Apple*, particularly in the face of rather glib chatter about the arts being commodified and artists turning into 'court jesters paid to pleasure visitors from the boardrooms of global capitalism'. But at the same time, money does talk; or, rather, in late capitalism, it murmurs quietly and insistently, and generally gets its bidding done through invisible, ideological coercion. Publishers, art dealers, and theatre managers, live by 'the market', and have become conditioned to know without thinking what sponsors will put up with, and what they won't.

In one of the most fascinating and provocative pieces here, a review of Douglas Murray's *Neoconservatism: Why We Need It*, Kevin teases out the bizarre facts surrounding Irving Kristol, the godfather of neoconservatism, who began political life as a Trotskyist but ended up as inspiration to the likes of Paul Wolfowitz and Richard Perle. It ends up partly agreeing with the title; the far left were wrong about bombing Bosnia, and the neocons were right. But it doesn't follow, therefore, that there is 'no doubt that Paul Wolfowitz and Richard Perle meant every word they said about wanting to bring democracy to Iraq. It was a noble and brave thing to want to do.' This, I think, is a necessary thing to say, and I was glad to have read it. The problem with most journalism is that we are so rarely forced by it to confront our own prejudices. Even so, I suspect that however much Wolfowitz and Perle 'wanted' democracy—why should they object to a 'democratic' Iraq, as long as it was USA-supporting?—they wanted other things far more. Among them was to intimidate Iran, secure oil supplies, and dispose of an uppity puppet dictator. None of which was said at the time. Nor did they give a damn about the hundreds of thousands of Iraqi civilian dead the invasion caused. So, 'Noble and brave'; no, never. This is one devil's advocacy that goes too far for its own good.

But the general point is easier to agree with: 'capitalist politicians in Ireland, or Britain, or the USA, may lie, but you will 'get over it', and may even 'vote them in again and live to tell the tale. However the lies the far Left tells are spiritually destructive, because they typically start out talking about a world of perfect human equality, before going on to say that to achieve this perfect world we must for now give "critical support" to this or that horrible tyrant.' Easier, because the attacks on the 'far left' surely stem in some measure from the sheer unforgivableness of their betrayal of the revolutionary aspirations he once held dear. It's hard to lose your faith in the secular utopia you and so many others once believed in. The review of *Koba the Dread* quotes some words of the elder Amis to his son: 'The Ideal of the brotherhood of man, the building of the Just City, is one that cannot be discarded without lifelong feelings of disappointment and loss.' Kevin adds: 'Now, this is a feeling which every disappointed socialist must at some time have felt. Once the possibility of a New Society has raised itself seriously in your head, then there really is no going back. As a friend of mine puts it: "Whatever you do, you can never unlearn all you now know to be wrong with the world. You can never just get on with things in the same way again."'

There are other alternatives to such 'disappointment' than those offered by Amis père, and it's just as well, but they're difficult to maintain. The hardest thing—harder than the handling the disappointment, really—is dealing with the hope that occasionally, irrepressibly, breaks through. It's like some failed love affair that just won't be laid to rest but keeps miserably flaring up. Isn't socialism well and truly defunct? Surely this is yet another tormenting false dawn, like all the rest? And yet it won't quite die. At this point I'd just note that the pieces in this entertaining, passionate and thoroughly thought-provoking book go back just over a decade. Remember the huge anti-globalization protests that started in Seattle in 1999? And how, in 2000, similar demonstrations challenged other get-togethers of the masters of the universe, at meetings of the IMF, the World Bank and the European Union? A major protest movement was developing; as one article points out: 'Politics of this sort was supposed to be a thing of the past. … The ladies and gentlemen who sit in the boardrooms of the global corporations can no longer expect to have everything their own way as easily as they did in the 80s and 90s, it must surely be time even the left's most ardent pessimists allowed something approaching a smile to flicker across their faces.' It's almost unbearably poignant that this is dated September 2001. We all know what happened next. 9/11 cut across the radical wave like a knife, nullifying it, and taking the flickering smile with it too. It's only now, perhaps, with the various protest encampments rippling out from Wall Street, general strikes in Greece and Italy, and the continuing Arab 'Spring', at the beginning of 2012, that we can dare to think we may be approaching a similar moment again.

So a decade has been lost; and yet still, perhaps, 'what does not change is the will to change', as Charles Olson wrote. A phrase associated with the Antonio Gramsci—one of the many more subtle Marxist thinkers the Tendency, predictably, never had time for—also comes to mind as the protest against the crisis swells: 'Pessimism of the intellect, optimism of the will'. Don't indulge in daydreams, but keep open at all costs a space in which the utopian imagination, in poetry as much as politics, can breathe. This sums up, it seems to me, Kevin Higgins's take on what lies ahead, which is ultimately an encouraging one. On the one hand, as he puts it, 'If you have no real answer, then far better to admit that rather than trying to bullshit your way to a unified theory of everything.' Which is bang on. Cultivate your garden. Don't force some procrustean mould down over the absurd richness of phenomena. But on the other, he foresees that the activity of the past few years is not going to vanish without trace either; some indelible mark has been made, new structures will grow, drawing in more of what lies around them, making new connections: 'I think that if the grassroots literary events which have grown so dramatically in the past few years all manage to keep going, and the signs are that they will, then they'll become forums where the tangible discontent and anger that's out there about what has happened and is going to happen will be given literary expression. This will especially be the case if we don't see emigration starting up again in a serious way, as it did during the 1980s. Either way, things will not be as they have been.'

JOHN GOODBY
Swansea, January 2012

John Goodby is the author of *Irish Poetry Since 1950: From Stillness Into History* (Manchester University Press)

Mentioning the War

Back Home to Ireland

I was just seven years old when we moved 'back home to Ireland' from Coventry in the English West Midlands during the summer of 1974. These days, when I remember Coventry, the pictures come in full colour: our hippie teacher, who sang Joni Mitchell songs and told us the meaning of big words, such as 'hypocrite'; my teddy-bear 'Sooty', lost forever during a train journey to Luton; the day I saw a worm wriggling up through the soil in our back garden and ran in screaming, telling my mother I'd seen a snake! And, of course, television. *The Magic Roundabout* and *Basil Brush*; *Dr. Who* and the daleks.

In the adult world these where times of upheaval. There were power cuts as the miners went on strike, not once but twice. It also saw the beginning of the IRA bombing campaign in Britain. A man was blown up by his own bomb at the nearby telephone exchange. I remember my father playing James Connolly and other rebel songs on the record player with the volume turned up full blast. But the closest this ugly adult stuff came to intruding on my small reality was when an episode of *Basil Brush* was cancelled to facilitate coverage of the February 1974 General Election. I remember indignantly asking my mother who 'those two Prime Minister men were?' She informed me that one of them was Ted Heath, the other Harold Wilson and suggested that I go outside and play.

I remember crying during dinnertime on my last day at school at The Sacred Heart on Harefield Road and being comforted by one of the girls in the class. It wasn't that I particularly liked school, more that, on some instinctive level, I could sense that this relatively happy chapter of my life was drawing to a close. The following Saturday we packed our belongings into a huge removal van and hit the motorway for Holyhead.

The pictures I have of Galway during the mid-nineteen seventies are all in black and white. I remember turning the television on, one afternoon, because it was time for *Sooty and Sweep*, but there was nothing on, nothing until the Angelus donged at six o'clock. I had landed in a country where children's television had yet to be invented. A bad situation was made even worse by the fact that in my Grandmother's house, where we spent those first few months, the television was always left off altogether as a mark of respect, whenever one of her elderly neighbours passed away, which they seemed to do with startling regularity. I was always mystified how these dead old people I'd never even met could possibly take me watching an episode of *Black Beauty* or *The Little House on the Prairie* as a mark of any sort of disrespect. But I thought it best not to argue.

We moved into the now demolished Rahoon flats just before Christmas 1974. There I watched the *Late Late Show* toy show for the very first time and things didn't seem so bad. In January 1975 I started at my new school, St. Pats. I was very frightened the first day because I didn't know anyone there. But I soon got used to it. We marched into class, two by two, three times every day and got the day off for De Valera's funeral. My mother said it was nice to see him going to his own funeral for a change.

I remember Galway footballers being so badly beaten in Sligo on a boiling hot day in 1975 that we ended up cheering for the other side. I remember eating chicken sandwiches in the backseat of the car as my father fixed yet another puncture. I remember the long drive home and learning to hate Sunday evenings.

A little later I remember being told to go over and touch Bishop Browne's cold dead hands as people filed past his casket in the Cathedral.

Broadcast on RTE Radio's *Sunday Miscellany*, July 2001

And no one knew its name

It all started the night before St. Patrick's Day, 1977. I must have been sound asleep at the time, because the first I heard of it was when I wandered into the kitchen early the following morning only to be told by my father that Mom wouldn't be able to come into town to watch the parade with the rest of us, as she usually did, because she'd been up most of the night with a pain in her back.

Having finally parcelled the three of us off to bed, she'd settled herself down with a hot whiskey to watch the special eve of St. Patrick's Day edition of *Trom agus Eadrom*. The Minister for the Gaeltacht, Mr. Tom O'Donnell T.D., was spluttering on as usual, like a character from *Hall's Pictorial Weekly*, when the pain suddenly hit and left her crying in agony on the living room floor of our corporation flat, number 270 Rahoon Park.

I didn't think much of it at the time. I tiptoed into Mom's bedroom, in case she might want a cup of tea or maybe a slice of toast. But she was fast asleep, so I left it at that. Helen and Ann-Marie would probably be a bit upset. They were both marching in the parade for the first time that year, with the Celine Hession School of Irish Dancing, and Mom wouldn't be there to get everything ready. But Dad would do his best. All would be well. Before we knew it, the parade would be over, and there'd be glasses of Coke and bags of crisps in The Imperial afterwards, when the Mayor had finally finished thanking the dignitaries, those strange men who always sat up high on the reviewing stand and, to me, looked suspiciously like tarted up TV licence inspectors, with their plug in smiles and new improved suits.

With a little more fuss than usual, Helen and Ann-Marie got their bits and pieces together and the four of us headed in towards the Square in my father's battered green Mini. Mom was still asleep when we left. The girls joined up with their marching group and we men stood and watched the parade with our serious faces and

27

folded arms. The parade was its usual pre-Macnas self. The lines of trucks carrying huge fridges and industrial machinery. The endless tin whistles. The majorettes "all the way from Boston, Massachusetts". The Irish dancers. Helen and Ann-Marie marching past the reviewing stand in their colourful uniforms. And, bringing up the rear, a small group of elderly Americans, all wearing golfing trousers and waving happily at everyone as they passed. Then came the speeches.

In 1977 the dignitary in the big picture was Minister for Posts and Telegraphs, Dr. Conor Cruise O'Brien. My father explained that he wasn't a doctor in the usual sense. You wouldn't go to him if you had a sore big toe or a boil on your backside. He had no interest in that sort of thing. He was a different sort of doctor altogether; the sort they usually keep hidden away down in the University, but in his case they had decided to make an exception and let him out for a while. Dr. O'Brien had, apparently, come to tell us about his big plan to give us more phones. One for everyone in the audience. To me, this all seemed very far fetched. And sure enough, when he stood up to speak, he talked instead about "the Provisional IRA". He seemed to be very angry about something and reminded me of one of my schoolteachers. He said that too many people had "an ambivalent attitude". I didn't know what this meant but I felt guilty all the same. He used loads of big words but, as far as I could tell, said nothing whatsoever about phones. Maybe it was all part of some big adult trick? Or maybe he'd been drinking? Drink sometimes made adults say the strangest things. Either way, I was glad when he finally stopped talking and sat back down.

Afterwards, The Imperial was so jam-packed we couldn't find a seat and so were forced to forgo our annual treat. We got a packet of crisps each instead to eat in the car and, on the way home, Helen pinched Ann-Marie, as she often did, and a fight ensued. They were still arguing about who had pulled whose hair first when Mom opened the front door. When they saw her face their fight was instantly forgotten. They skipped inside chirping excitedly about everything and anything. It had been a strange sort of day, but at least now things seemed to be settling back into an easier rhythm.

However, as Mom's back pain returned, again and again, over the days and weeks that followed things bore less and less of a resemblance to the normality I'd previously known. Sometimes it would stay away for as long as a week or two. But it always returned; when we were visiting my Grandparents, when we were in town, when we were on the bus…The only predictable thing about it was that it could arrive at any time of the day or night. My abiding memory of the Spring and early Summer of 1977 is of my mother's increasingly agonised screams as it took possession of her, time after time. A new invisible enemy had taken its place in our lives. And no one knew its name.

She did the rounds of the doctors and specialists. At first, everyone presumed she had a slipped disc, but when they x-rayed her spine, everything looked fine. So there was nothing for them to fix. But the pain kept coming, like missiles whistling through a clear blue sky. She went to see a special 'bone-doctor' down in Tipperary and he told her that there was nothing whatsoever wrong with her back. In desperation, people began to suggest the names of various faith healers.

The memories I have of that summer are vivid. My previously lukewarm support for Liverpool Football Club developed into an absolute obsession, as the season drew to a close and they moved tantalisingly towards a possible treble of League Championship, F.A. and European Cups. I was absolutely heartbroken when, on the second Saturday in May, they lost by two goals to one to Manchester United in the F.A. Cup Final. I watched the whole sorry tale unfold on our crackly black and white TV. But the following Wednesday I was ecstatic when they defeated the German champions, Borussia Monchengladbach by three goals to one to become European Champions for the first time. It was Kevin Keegan's last match for Liverpook and he played brilliantly. They were already leading 2-1 with only minutes to go when he got the ball yet again and seemed to be heading straight for the German goal until Bertie Vogts brought him down, well inside the penalty area. Phil Neal slotted the ensuing penalty into the net and that was that.

A few weeks later I saw a book called *Liverpool's March to European Glory* up on a shelf in O'Gorman's Bookshop. I leafed through it, glancing at the pictures. I simply had to have it. But it was expensive. And I only had twenty five pence. So instead of buying it, I decided to borrow it without asking their permission. I was very nervous as I sneaked out the door, with the book bulging through my jacket, trying not to look suspicious. The book was brilliant; its pages shiny with loads of photographs. After that I borrowed a few more books and comics from the same shop. It was so easy. But, for some reason, my life of crime ended there. I was probably afraid of getting caught. And the truth was, that if Mom had been her usual self, I'd never have gotten away with it in the first place. She'd have kept asking where I was getting all those books and comics. I'd have been forced to make up loads of lies about having borrowed them from various people at school. But she'd have taken one look at them with their shiny new covers and high prices and wouldn't have believed a word of it. The old Mom always caught me out when I was telling lies.

If May was the month of Liverpool, Kevin Keegan and the European Cup, June was the month of the 'landslide'. A General Election was held and the old government got so badly beaten that adults everywhere kept describing it as a landslide. It was so bad that Dr. O'Brien, he of the non-existent phones and "Provisional IRA", lost his seat. They showed him talking on the television. He seemed to be even angrier than when he had come to talk to us on St. Patrick's Day. I wondered what would become of him now.

By then we were off school for the summer holidays. But Mom was no better and the Doctors still didn't know what was wrong. Some even seemed to think that she was making it all up. "Psychosomatic", they called it. At the end of June they finally took her into hospital. She spent six weeks on "traction" in Merlin Park. They kept her in bed all day with weights hanging from her legs, in the vague hope that this might somehow make her better. Merlin Park was an unusual hospital in that it wasn't just one big building, like most hospitals, but was divided into loads of little buildings. "Units", they called them. I visited her at least two or three times a week. The pain kept coming and they started to give her pain killing injections, which were so strong they sometimes knocked her out.

Around this time her mother came to visit her, which was something of a special occasion, because my Grandmother suffered from her "nerves" and hardly ever came to visit anybody. She told Mom that it was terrible the Doctors couldn't find a cure for either of them, which was a bit strange given the fact that Mom was sick and she wasn't. Mom said that it was best just to ignore her, to "offer it up", because Granny was one of those people who thought that hospitals should only be used by her.

Mom was home again by early August. I remember sitting beside her on the couch when the news came over that Elvis Presley had died. I had heard of him but, at first, couldn't see what all the fuss was about. The following day she bought several newspapers and read everything they said about him. She told me how she was always trying to listen to his songs years ago on *Radio Luxembourg* and my grandmother was always trying to stop her, which didn't surprise me in the least. As August waned and the dreaded return to school loomed, a parcel arrived in a brown cardboard box from America. It was from our Aunt in Chicago and contained pages and pages of magazine articles about Elvis as well as a pair of yellow trousers, which I hoped I'd never have to wear.

September arrived and wasn't content to be its usual miserable self. It hit us like ice tearing the side of a ship. I was only back at school two days when Mom was taken back into hospital. They still didn't know what was wrong. The pain was worse than ever and now she was losing weight as well. I remember very little about the following few months. I have hazy memories of visiting Mom in hospital. I remember them sticking a needle in her arm as they put her on a "drip" and that Liverpool got off to a rotten start in the new football season.

My next really vivid memory is of Mom coming home from hospital on Christmas Eve. We all went out to collect her in the battered green Mini. On our way back we had to stop off at the Shopping Centre because we hadn't been to see Santa yet. By then Mom was so sick she wasn't even able to get out of the car, so she waited there while Dad ushered us quickly in and out. The fake Santa with his cotton wool beard gave me a small plastic motorbike with a little man sitting on it. It was exactly the same as the one he'd given me the previous year.

But I got a lovely pair of football boots the following morning. Wearing them I could pretend to be Kevin Keegan or Kenny Dalglish. And that's exactly what I did that Christmas morning as I kicked a football up and down the road, which ran up to Rahoon flats. It's strange to pass there now, almost twenty five years later, and see that road where I kicked that football still almost intact. They left it there when they knocked the flats and sometimes, on Sundays, I see other boys kicking other footballs as I go past.

Mom spent most of Christmas in bed. She did get up for Christmas dinner but wasn't able to eat very much and went back to bed immediately afterwards. By now she weighed less than five stone, was suffering from terrible night sweats and having bad dreams. On St. Stephen's Day we took her back to hospital. I'll never forget her standing there at the door of Merlin Park Hospital, Unit 6, slowly disappearing as we drove away in total silence. I still didn't know what was happening. And I had no idea where this would end. I just knew that things were getting worse.

We went back to school in January. And I accompanied Dad to my grandfather's anniversary mass. Old women nodded knowingly and seemed to take pity on me. As the priest spoke I remembered Granddad dead in his coffin. It was horrible. Him all emaciated and his face twisted by the sickness. Stomach cancer they called it. I spent the entire journey back to Galway trying to get that picture out of my head, but whatever I did, I could think of nothing else.

That same evening they put Mom in an ambulance and moved her across town from Merlin Park to the Regional. When I heard the news I thought "well at least now I can visit her on my way home from school". And they'd given her a room of her own as well, which was much better than having to share with all those old ladies out in Merlin Park, with their bad hips and broken legs. However, during her first week in the Regional, her room seemed always to be full of adults, doctors and nurses whispering to each other about blood tests and "biopsies". Something seemed to be happening. But, of course, no one told me what it was.

Until one day, when I went to see her after school—it was a Tuesday and I had brought her a copy of *The Connacht Sentinel*— Mom told me that the invisible enemy finally had a name. She was suffering from something called Hodgkin's Disease. This meant nothing to me, but a name is a name and, however long it took, I'd get used to saying it. She said that there was something wrong with her blood. She kept describing it as a "second cousin to Leukaemia". It wasn't her back at all. Everything made a little more sense all of a sudden. Now they could, at long last, give her some proper treatment. She was to have her first treatment the following day and seemed to be looking forward to it. As I walked home up Seamus Quirke Road, I was happier than I had been for months. But I couldn't help wondering who Hodgkin was? And what had he done to have such a horrible thing named after him? I hoped that no one would ever call a disease after me.

The weeks that followed were dominated by Mom getting her regular blasts of chemotherapy. The stuck loads of needles in her veins and pumped medicine into her in an effort to kill the diseased cells. Once the diseased ones were dead, other healthy ones would grow in their place. Or at least that was the idea. The treatment seemed to make her both worse and better at the same time. Afterwards, she always got sick. Usually several times. But she began to put on weight and to look much better in between treatments.

The day she came home from hospital was the best day ever. She was sitting on a chair in the kitchen when I got home from school. It was only February but the sun had come out again. She never had to go back to live in a hospital again. She still had to have her treatments. Once a fortnight at first. Then once a month for a year. Each time getting sick into the kitchen sink. I remember asking her if all this getting sick was really good for her? But, this time, the Doctors seemed to know what they were doing. She had her last treatment in the Spring of 1979, just before we moved into our new house where she still lives. They told her that she was in something known as "remission". I asked her if that was good or bad and she told me that it was good, very good indeed.

Criterion magazine, February 2002

Walter Macken—Dreams On Paper

by Ultan Macken

When I was a teenager my dad once or twice said: "you'll be one of those *literary* types, like that fella Walter Macken." This wasn't, I'm pretty sure, intended as a compliment, but rather a reaction to what he perceived as an aversion on my part to heavy physical labour. It was the first time I had heard of Walter Macken, the person; before that his name evoked not books but the corporation flats named after him in Mervue. From then on the words 'Walter Macken' meant writer, because he was the first writer I'd heard talked about as being a real person who lived in the actual place that was the Galway of his time. Before that I had no idea that there was any such thing as a "literary type".

This biography by his son Ultan is based largely on Macken's letters, both those he wrote to others and those he received. The letters are mostly included in full, rather than extracted. Some other family correspondence is also used; the final letter here is one sent to the author by his mother, Peggy, on April 12th 1967, ten days before Walter Macken died of a massive heart attack at his home in Menlo at the age of just fifty two. The first chapter 'Grandfather Macken—His Life And Times' is based on the letters of Walter Macken's own father, also Walter, who was killed in the First World War, when his son was still less than a year old. The first sentence of the official letter from the Chaplain of his regiment informing his wife of his death reads: "I am writing to tell you that your husband, 18092, Pt W. Macken of this regiment was almost certainly killed on March 28th, [1916] though his name will appear as missing, I cannot give you any particulars."

Ultan Macken's technique of interspersing these letters with his own commentary works well and gives the reader the sense that he is getting at, if not the whole truth—no biography can do that—then at least some good part of it. The fact that his tone is in places decidedly unsentimental also helps, sentimentality being the deadliest danger in a book such as this. When a writer claims to have had a childhood that was seamless in its wonderfulness, and goes on to say that his or her parents were both great people who never made any mistakes, no one with a brain believes it. I was particularly interested to read Walter Macken's own account of his time spent attending the Patrician Brothers' National School between 1922 and 1927:

> "I remember playing crowded football in the concrete yard, lacerated knees and the seagulls over the river beyond the railings where we fed them with our bits of bread while they performed flying gymnastics as they screamed and called. It was hard leaving the seagulls for the classroom. I remember the class being dominated by the thought of Brother Joseph in Sixth Class. We could hear him in the room over our heads each year as we progressed. He believed in noisy punishment, the sounds of which haunted us, but as dreams cannot live up to reality, neither can nightmares. Things were not as bad as they sounded, when we got there."

Later in the book Ultan Macken discusses the difficulties both he and his parents had when his brother Wally Óg joined Opus Dei during his last year at school. The family was strongly religious and "there was no doubt that he had a religious vocation." It had been presumed that Wally Óg would become a priest; but most members of Opus Dei did not. Opus Dei was, as Ultan Macken says, "founded by a young Spanish Priest, José Maria Escriva in the 1930s in direct opposition to the Communist Party who were actively recruiting young people all over Spain." Its origins were clearly fascist; several members of Opus Dei served in General Franco's government. Opus Dei has been accused of using cultish methods, and there is evidence of such methods here. After his brother formally joined the organisation in March 1956, Ultan Macken says: "I became like an only child." And on May 29th 1956, in a letter to his American cousin, Sabina, Walter Macken wrote: "Wally Óg only partly belongs to us now—he is not permitted to come on holidays with us (I will explain this mysterious statement when we meet)".

In 1962 Wally Óg was ordained as a priest. His parents were both delighted with this and travelled to his ordination in Spain. One of their big reservations about Opus Dei seems, from Ultan Macken's account, to have been that they thought membership of it would likely prevent Wally Óg from becoming a priest.

As well as telling the story of the Macken family, *Dreams On Paper* also provides us with valuable insights into Walter Macken's career as a writer. He began to write at the age of eight. At twelve "he had already written quite a lot and decided to submit a short story to *The Daily Telegraph*. He was disgusted when they returned his story to him, having rejected it." A key question for any writer is what to do with his of her disgust. Macken kept working at it, chanced into a job at the Taibhdhearc Theatre where he was introduced to both what is sometimes called the 'arts community' and his future wife, Peggy Kenny. She was a writer in her own right, a journalist with, and later editor of, *The Connacht Tribune*.

Ultan Macken tells us: "My father had a stated plan and he stuck rigidly by it—to write a play in English and then tackle a novel." Though the word 'writer' may for some conjure up the image of pale figures in battered velvet jackets who spend their days drinking absinthe in Montmartre or pints in Neachtains, most people who actually write anything tend to have some version of Macken's "stated plan". During the 1940s Macken established a writing routine which would be his modus operandi for the rest of his life: "He always wrote in the morning and he went to work at the theatre in the afternoon." On October 18th 1946 Macken submitted his completed first play to the Abbey Theatre for their consideration. Ernest Blythe replied. He asked Macken to change the title of the play from 'Mungo and the Mowleogs' to *Mungo's Mansion*. That aside, yes, the Abbey were interested in premiering his play. *Mungo's Mansion* was then accepted for publication by Macmillan in London. As any writer could tell you, such initial breakthroughs are hugely important.

Macken immediately sent Macmillan a novel he had been working on, then titled 'Wise Men of Blood, O God'. After much agonised waiting for their reply, several title changes, and serious revision of the original manuscript, his first novel, *Quench The Moon*, was published in 1948. From there on came the usual mix of disappointment, occasional triumph and money worries that mark most writers' lives. The Galway Walter Macken wrote about is lost to us now, and we wouldn't have it back. But his struggle then was, in every important way, the same one anyone who wants to make writing his or her life faces today.

Socialist Classics

George Orwell, *Homage to Catalonia*

A couple of years ago, while in Athens to give a poetry reading with some other Irish poets, I got into a conversation with an elderly Englishman, there to translate into English the work of a group of Greek poets who were reading their work at the same event. The littlest of men, throughout our stay he always wore jumpers which, set against his tiny frame, were so enormous he appeared to be permanently in danger of disappearing into them. His voice never rose to much more than a very distinguished whisper. One morning we wandered onto the subject of George Orwell. He said that he "never did get" what he described as "the Orwell thing". Orwell was someone who had "done a bit of the bohemian thing, then dabbled in a bit of the political thing, before reverting to type. I never have seen what all the fuss is about," he told me. Later, after the poetry reading was over, we all went to an American-style bar which had a DJ who played music from the 1960s and '70s. After a glass or two of Ouzo, said Englishman in his jumper turned to me, pointed at a picture of Jimi Hendrix on the wall and, struggling to be heard above the music, told me: "I once got a ticket to go and see that young man play at some festival on the Isle of Wight. I ended up not going, because there was a political meeting I felt I really shouldn't miss. It's always annoyed me a bit, because the Communist Party event I went to instead turned out to be a bloody boring affair."

George Orwell is the writer even the most cultured Stalinists can never really forgive. And *Homage to Catalonia* (1938) is the book of his which really soured that relationship. In his previous book *The Road to Wigan Pier* (1937) he had certainly been critical of Communist Party types: "shock-haired Marxists chewing polysyllables". And at a time when so many had illusions in the

Soviet Union, Orwell talked instead about "Bolshevik commissars (half gangster, half gramophone)". In *Homage to Catalonia*, though, George Orwell crossed not one but two rubicons which ensured that, whatever other justified criticisms may be levelled at him, he would amount to much more than just another literary gent who flirted with radicalism in his youth before reverting to type and turning into another Kingsley Amis or John Osborne or Malcolm Muggeridge.

In *Homage to Catalonia* Orwell for the first time puts himself on the side of revolution, the overthrow of capitalism rather than its gradual reform. In its description of Barcelona at the height of the revolution, the book gives us some of the most inspirational words ever set down on paper by a convinced socialist, far superior to the more leaden reportage that characterises a book such as *Ten Days That Shook The World*:

> Almost my first experience was receiving a lecture for trying to tip a lift-boy. There were no private motor cars, they had all been commandeered, and all the trams and taxis were painted red and black. The revolutionary posters were everywhere, flaming from the walls in clean reds and blues that made the few remaining advertisements look like daubs of mud. Down the Ramblas, the wide central artery of the town where crowds of people streamed constantly to and fro, the loudspeakers were bellowing revolutionary songs all day and far into the night. And it was the aspect of the crowds that was queerest of all. In outward appearance it was a town in which the wealthy classes had practically ceased to exist. Except for a small number of women and foreigners there were no 'well-dressed' people at all. Practically everyone wore rough working-class clothes, or blue overalls or some variant of the militia uniform. All this was queer and moving. There was much in it that I did not understand, in some ways I did not even like it, but I recognised it immediately as a state of affairs worth fighting for.

As Orwell himself admits, there's much not to like here. I don't own a car, but know a lot of people who do. and don't think they'd be much taken with the idea of having their vehicles commandeered by not very well-dressed anarchists and assorted reds. And as for "loudspeakers... bellowing revolutionary songs all day and far into the night", I find that since I turned forty I like that sort of carry-on less and less. It has something to do with having to get up for work in the morning. There is, though, a great sense of freedom and possibility in this scene of revolution as described by Orwell, a sense that, despite the terrible inconvenience of their world having been turned upside down, people believed they were witnessing the birth of something much better than the Barcelona that used to be, where everyone knew his or her place and addressed the master as 'Señor' or 'Don'. All of that is gone. In the new Barcelona no one appears to either defer to or look down on anyone else. A state of affairs worth fighting for, most certainly.

Orwell very soon realised that what he encountered was a society in transition rather than one in which capitalism had been decisively overthrown: "great numbers of well-to-do bourgeois were simply lying low and disguising themselves as proletarians for the time being". Just a few months later, things had slid backwards: "Now things were returning to normal. The smart restaurants and hotels were full of rich people wolfing expensive meals, while for the working-class population food prices had jumped enormously without any corresponding rise in wages." Of course the Communist Party, which gained disproportionate influence because the Soviet Union was the only country to provide military aid to the Spanish republic, was advocating a Popular Front against fascism. The Popular Front, as well as including social democrats and Stalinists, was also attempting to appeal to the 'liberal bourgeois'. The Irish equivalents would probably be the likes of Vincent Browne, Fintan O'Toole and Mary Robinson. Such people tend to like good restaurants, and also to get decidedly queasy when anyone suggests abolishing the Seán Fitzpatricks and Michael O'Learys of this world, rather than merely reforming them and holding them to account by giving Dáil committees more power. An Irish version of the Spanish Popular Front would probably see a left unity government appointing Fintan O'Toole to the Seanad and giving Vincent Browne a special restaurant allowance in the hope that both might write nice things about them in *The Irish Times*.

In *Homage to Catalonia* Orwell, whose *Animal Farm* was later co-opted by the CIA, writes from a position that is decisively to the left not only of the Labour Party but also of the Communist Party. He is for the revolution to a far greater extent than Pablo Neruda, André Malraux, Stephen Spender, W H Auden, Cecil Day Lewis and all Stalinism's literary fellow travellers ever were.

Having crossed the rubicon that separates reform and revolution, what happened next was in the context inevitable. It is clear that Orwell's undying hatred of the Communist Party was born in Spain. Before Spain he tended to view individual Stalinists, particularly the intellectual types with their jargon and lack of any obvious connection to or empathy for the working class, as another variant of the English eccentric. In *The Road To Wigan Pier* he wrote of how the working class member of the CP was always the least orthodox, capable of both attending mass and reading *The Daily Worker*. Here, his profound mistrust of Stalinism is transformed into hatred. Orwell had a relationship with the truth which means that this was probably always going to happen. He lacked the ability to look the other way in order to avoid inconvenient truths which so many left-leaning writers are expert at. It became obvious to him the Communist Party was actually in the process of derailing the revolution which had been provoked by General Franco's attempted coup in 1936. The CP leadership would rather Franco win than have a successful revolution in Spain which they did not control:

> on every wall the Government agents had stencilled: 'We need a Popular Army,' and over the radio and in the Communist Press there was a ceaseless and sometimes very malignant jibing against the militias, who were described as ill-trained, undisciplined, etc. etc.; the Popular Army was always described as 'heroic'. From much of the propaganda you would have derived the impression that there was something disgraceful in having gone to the front voluntarily and something praiseworthy in waiting to be conscripted.

Some socialists see *Homage to Catalonia* as the highpoint of Orwell's commitment to socialism and contrast its apparent optimism favourably with the darkly pessimistic *Nineteen Eighty-Four*, published ten years later. It is certainly true that most of the anti-Communist cold warriors who after the second world war became big fans of Orwell's final two novels, *Animal Farm* (published in 1945) and *Nineteen Eighty-Four*, had little use for *Homage to Catalonia*. It's hard, for example, to imagine Hollywood making a film of it, as it did of *Animal Farm*, albeit with a tacked-on Disney-style ending. It would have become a little too obvious that, faced with the political choices then on offer in Spain, the studio moguls would have chosen General Franco.

But without his experience in Spain, *Animal Farm* and *Nineteen Eighty-Four* could never have been written. The rats in *Nineteen Eighty-Four's* Room 101 are said not to be the product of Orwell's imagination but of an account related to Orwell by his friend Georges Kopp, who was arrested during the Communist-inspired crackdown against Andrés Nin's party of non-Stalinist socialists, the POUM. Kopp was in prison for eighteen months where he was interrogated by NKVD agents. He was later nursed back to health in England by relatives of Orwell. Remember now, Kopp was fighting on the *same* side as the Communists who imprisoned and tortured him. The next time a big meeting is called, the purpose of which is to get all the left wing groups to forget their differences and come together in united socialist loveliness, remember his name and then watch *that* scene from the film version of *Nineteen Eighty-Four.* Then you'll be ready to attend said meeting with something approaching a realistic idea of what you might be getting into.

Elsewhere in *Nineteen Eighty-Four*, O'Brien of the Thought Police cheerily tells his captive Winston Smith: "If you want a picture of the future, imagine a boot stamping on a human face—forever." This was inspired by an anti-POUM poster which Orwell observed all around Barcelona as the Stalinists cracked down on their opponents on the left. It showed POUM 'fifth columnist' traitors being stamped on by a very willing Communist boot. During this period Orwell spent several days effectively on the run in Barcelona, with his wife Eileen waiting back at the hotel for him. Orwell's association with the POUM was accidental. At the outset of the war he had naively gone to see Harry Pollitt, general secretary of the Communist Party of Great Britain, to ask if he could help him get to Spain. Pollitt was suspicious of Orwell, and refused. Orwell's next stop was the Independent Labour Party, who put him in touch with the POUM.

Despite the terrible things he'd witnessed and the fact that he was badly wounded fighting fascists on the front line in the early days of the war, Orwell left Spain in an optimistic state of mind:

> When you have had a glimpse of such a disaster as this—and however it ends the Spanish war will turn out to have been an appalling disaster, quite apart from the slaughter and physical suffering—the result is not necessarily disillusionment and

disaster. Curiously enough the whole experience has left me with not less but more belief in the decency of human beings.

In everyday terms, this might seem like madness. But Orwell was a man inspired by what he had seen of Spain's actually existing revolution in its best early days. No longer was socialism an abstract idea—the preserve of "shock-haired Marxists chewing polysyllables"—it was now a street he had actually walked down. After that everything else was an anticlimax:

> For months we had been telling ourselves that 'when we get out of Spain' we would go somewhere beside the Mediterranean and be quiet for a while and perhaps do a little fishing; but now we were here it was merely a bore and a disappointment... It sounds like lunacy, but the thing that both of us wanted was to be back in Spain... both of us wished that we had stayed to be imprisoned along with the others.

Things as they actually were in France and England, as he journeyed home with Eileen, were inevitably a disappointment after the glimpse he'd had in Barcelona of things as they could be.

Red Banner magazine, June 2011

Elaine Feeney: One of Ireland's Growing Band of Young Political Poets

I know Cúirt's new programme director, Dani Gill, was determined that this year's festival should not be dominated by recycled names from previous years. The inclusion of Elaine Feeney, whose first collection of poems *Where's Katie?* was published by Salmon last year, is proof that this is indeed Cúirt made new.

Feeney was born in Galway in 1979 and is one of a group of young political poets—others would include Dave Lordan and Sarah Clancy—who have sprung to prominence recently. They share a declamatory style of reading their poems. Her dramatic and witty and very appealing reading style won Feeney the Cúirt Poetry Grand Slam in 2008. Her winning poem, 'Urban Myths and the Galway Girl', is a favourite in the justifiably acclaimed *Where's Katie?*: "Everywhere in Galway waters down her vodka. / She'll tell Pauline that Christine is a wench / she'll tell Christine that Pauline is loose./ She tells me about all the pills the husband is taking / for the cough and the limp dick and all / nothing is working / loveeeen." The main inspiration which brought about this poem appears to have been real people talking rubbish. In this, Feeney's is an example other poets might like to consider following. So often, the poetry is all around you in the form of the truly incredible things people actually say, and all you need to do is write it down.

Herself, Lordan and Clancy also share radical leftist politics of slightly varying shades. All three have signed up to support a cultural boycott of Israel by Irish artists. This is a stance I wouldn't be at all convinced of myself. Not because I'm any fan of the way the Israeli state has abused and continues to abuse the Palestinians. But rather because it puts the well meaning in dodgy political company, inevitably including one or two who think of Colonel

Ghaddafi as some kind of anti-imperialist. However, Feeney's poem 'Gaza', in which she makes imaginative reference to William Carlos Williams' 'The Red Wheelbarrow', is a powerful statement on a subject fraught with cliché. Its end is stark: "Snap. // The little girl drops like // the plastic bullets all around her, / slumps on her wheelbarrow, / upon which so much depended."

While Elaine Feeney cut her teeth as a poet at events such as North Beach Poetry Nights during those couple of really crazy years before the crash; her poetry is ideally suited to the angrier, more politically engaged country we have woken up in to find not just the party over, but all future parties cancelled. That said, there is more to her than anger. In 'Love' she says "If Love were served as a mojito with ice, / I would shove its leaves / to the recess of my throat / and beg for mercy." Something about this image of Feeney throwing back a Mojito humanises her anger and makes the reader listen all the more intently. Elaine Feeney will be reading alongside young Slovenian novelist Goran Vojnovic at the Druid Lane Theatre on Wednesday, April 13th, 1pm.

Galway Advertiser, April 2011

Game Of Golf That Brought Down A Government

The Fitzpatrick Tapes—The rise and fall of one man, one bank and one country by TOM LYONS & BRIAN CAREY

On Monday, July 28th, 2008 Sean Fitzpatrick played eighteen holes of golf with Brian Cowen on Druid's Heath at the foot of the Wicklow mountains. Afterwards they had dinner at the resort's hotel. When asked what himself and Brian Cowen talked about Fitzpatrick says: "The world, Ireland, the economy." He's quick to add that they did not talk about "Anglo Irish Bank or anything like that." Given the crisis at Anglo Irish was underway at this point—its share price having been under attack since St. Patrick's Day—and that Cowen had been made aware of the problem caused by Sean Quinn's acquisition of a large stake in the bank and subsequent need to offload a huge number of shares all at once, it seems incredible that Cowen didn't once ask how things were going at Anglo. Like the captain of the Titanic, he let the ship keep going in the same direction until the Irish banking system was ripped apart by the icebergs of September. Two months later the bank guarantee was introduced and ever since Irish capitalism has been reliant on the charity of the European Central Bank.

One thing Cowen and Fitzpatrick had in common as they golfed their way around the greens was a dangerous tendency to be taken in by their own propaganda. Both swallowed whole the free market fundamentalism, which was born with Thatcher and Reagan and died the day Lehman's went bust, and appear never to have considered the possibility of a 1929 style crash. Fitzpatrick admits to having been blindsided by the anger waiting for him when he returned from South Africa after taking a holiday there after his resignation as Chairman of Anglo: "[A named colleague] had rung me. He said…If I were you I wouldn't come home to this f***ing kip…I said, Don't be ridiculous. He said, I am serious, it's terrible. I just didn't believe him."

Fitzpatrick is too charming by half and, whatever he did in life, was perhaps destined to lead some group of gullibles over a cliff. Given the closeness of Cowen's relationship with Fitzpatrick, the final accusation our soon to be former Taoiseach must face is that of cronyism: that Anglo Irish Bank was a Fianna Fáil bank and that's why he was determined to save it whatever the expense. Yes, Cowen appears to have believed that the sun shone out of Seanie. And it's clear now that it didn't. But this story reeks of cock-up rather than conspiracy. Similarly, the idea that Fianna Fáil is the sole practitioner of political cronyism doesn't stand up to examination. When Des Geraghty was appointed to the board of the Financial Regulator last year, having only recently resigned from the board of our other national disaster, FAS, no one from the Labour Party, of which Geraghty is a member, had a word to say about this rather odd appointment. Joe Higgins recently came out in support of former Scottish Socialist leader, Tommy Sheridan, who was jailed last week for perjuring himself during a libel action he took against the *News of The World*, which had published a story about Sheridan attending orgies at a 'swingers club'. For once the *News of The World* was telling the truth. Joe's statement talked about Sheridan having been "singled out" because he was "a consistent fighter against the neo liberal policies". Indeed. Even if Fianna Fáil loses every single seat in the upcoming election, political cronyism will remain alive and well in Ireland. The evidence is all around you, on any part of the political spectrum you care to examine.

Galway Advertiser, February 2011

The Ballad of Shell and Rossport

Once Upon A Time In The West: The Corrib Gas Controversy
by Lorna Siggins

To say that the Shell gas pipeline and terminal in North Mayo has been the subject of controversy would be to understate seriously. To those not directly involved, the ongoing 'debate', which has regularly degenerated into violence with allegations of intimidation on both sides, has often seemed, like Northern Ireland in the seventies, to be one where it's difficult to give either side unqualified support. This could be said to mark a failure on the part of the Shell To Sea campaign; another case of the right side losing because it puts its argument histrionically rather than rationally and allows some to be spokespersons for the campaign who'd be better kept in the background, stapling placards or making sandwiches for visiting protestors. The ranting boys and girls of *The Sunday Independent* have been happy to do their bit to blacken the reputation of Shell To Sea. The 'documentary' by Paul Williams, aired on TV3 last year, which tried to paint the campaign as being the plaything of dissident republicans, was the sort of rag journalism one would expect from someone who now writes for the *News of The World*.

Lorna Siggins is a different kind of journalist and works with facts rather than bar stool opinions of either variety. On page 215 she speaks to Sarah Clancy from Galway about violence Clancy personally witnessed being meted out to protesters by Gardaí. Now, while I doubt that myself and Sarah vote the same way at elections, I believe her when she says that she observed a Shell To Sea protester "being flung to the ground, with 'first two, then one garda kneeling on his back" as they "pressed his face into the dirt, all the while hitting him with batons". There were at least four

Gardaí involved in this, Clancy says. This is not to paint the campaign as a bunch of angels. I know from personal experience that there are those of the activist left who are willing to use physical intimidation as a tactic and others who are willing to make excuses for such behaviour. In *Once Upon A Time In The West*, Siggins makes an angel of no one.

The facts she has gathered lead her to be more sympathetic to the protesters than she is to *Shell*. That as neutral an observer as Lorna Siggins could come to this view should give middle Ireland pause. If it is true, as Shell To Sea claim, that a natural resource worth hundreds of billions of Euro has been more or less given away to *Shell* with very little benefit to the Irish exchequer, then it is a very serious matter indeed. If the Shell To Sea protesters are even half right, then there certainly could have been, and perhaps still is, an alternative to slashing social welfare and services to the disabled and all the other miseries the Colm McCarthys and Peter Sutherlands are currently prescribing for us. Go out tomorrow and buy this book. You can't afford not to.

Galway Advertiser, November 2010

Culture and the recession

Since the implosion of the international banking system in September 2008 ushered in this era of our great economic unhappiness, the atmosphere of everyday life in Ireland has changed for everybody to an extent that would have been unimaginable just three years ago. Be you nurse, property developer, teacher, banker, person with disabilities, administrator of corrupt FÁS scheme, teenager sitting the Leaving Cert or Fianna Fáil politician in search of votes, nothing is quite as it was during the dear departed era of bigger, better, faster, more. This is not to say that we are all in it together. But whoever you are, the age of less is upon you.

You will be forced to pay for the clean-up, whether or not you got to go to the party during those years when each July the sky right above me was loud with helicopters carrying Seánie and Dunner and Fingers and friends to the Galway Races. The G Hotel out the road used to charge €2,500 per night for its luxury suite during race week. This year no one, with the exception of Ireland's foremost stand-up comedian Enda Kenny, wants to be seen dead with the fallen gods of the property bubble. Last month one Galway establishment received seven hundred applications for a few badly-paid jobs collecting glasses for the week of the festival. Many people are desperate. Property developers and bankers have now joined paedophile priests at the bottom of most people's invitation list for any event at which other human beings will be present. To paraphrase Leonard Cohen: it's been a long way down. Such disturbed economic weather has inevitably had a big effect on the arts, particularly at the grassroots level. I took part in a night of poetry and music at the International Bar in Dublin recently which had something of the atmosphere of the Weimar Republic about it. The capacity crowd was a little on the raucous side, but very friendly with the exception of one inebriated gentlemen of middling years who had to be escorted to the exit because he kept interrupting the performers. He repeatedly muttered, rather disconcertingly, that he had "something to say about Christopher Hitchens"!

For most of the nineties and noughties such an individual would have been seen by many younger audience members as an unshaven throwback to the grim and dirty days of the mid-1980s: one of life's losers who, though the whole world around him was now winning, was still working hard to continue the losing streak which probably began the day Horslips broke up. He's the kind of guy who typically likes an economic crisis because it provides him with a background into which he can partly fade. Paradoxically, despite the fact that he was shown the door and I was one of the guest poets, I felt he fitted in with the crowd, many of whom felt sorry for him, at least as much I did. The motto 'There but for the grace of whoever could go any of us' is back, which is maybe a first step back towards something like solidarity. So many people are losing these days, the word 'loser' is likely on its way to join 'property ladder' and 'soft landing' in the dustbin of terms that no longer apply. The 'Show me the money, fuck you, I want it now' vibe of pre-2008 is as dead and gone as the Fianna Fáil tent.

The cultural scene is also undergoing big changes, although I can only speak in detail about my own area, literature. As with the economy, it looks very much like the 1930s in slow motion. The big festivals which a couple of years back would pay healthy fees to visiting poets and fiction writers are coming under pressure. This year Mayo County Council's Arts Office cancelled their popular Force 12 Writers Weekend in Belmullet, apparently for financial reasons. In the summer of 2008, when the word 'recession' had just crept back into the lexicon of Irish pub talk but before Lehman Brothers went belly up, a group of us were well paid to read our work and conduct workshops at said festival. It was for many years a great gathering point for writers—both established and new—in the west. Its demise is a great pity, and just one example of how the crisis is making life narrower and duller for many. This is not intended to be any sort of criticism of those who work for Mayo County Council Arts Office. It is easy to mouth empty, left-sounding criticisms of arts 'bureaucrats'. Such rants are rarely anything like the truth, and taking them at face value will only lead you into the company of some of the worst cranks imaginable. The cranks who loiter on the fringes of the arts are typically even worse than the most ghastly political crank you've ever met on the left. Although, in a few cases, they save us time by actually being the same people.

The truth is that those responsible for the arts in every local authority countrywide, and administrators in a wide variety of established arts organisations, have since the onset of the recession been moving heaven and earth and then some to try and ensure that the arts and personal creativity can remain accessible to as many people as possible in all the many forms that might take. This will on occasion mean trying to rustle up the funds to ensure that an opera festival continues or that an exhibition of abstract art can go ahead. Some would say that such elitist minority interests should not receive public money. But the truth is that far more of what the left likes to call 'ordinary working class people' attended the Galway Arts Festival this July, for example, than will this year or next year attend all the public meetings of the different Irish far left groups put together. Facts like this should give you pause next time your inner philistine asks why on earth taxpayers should be subsidising such things at a time when tens of thousands of workers are losing their jobs and services such as health and education are being slashed.

The entire budget for both the Arts Council and Culture Ireland, which offers grants to help promote the work of Irish artists to audiences outside Ireland, was €73.23 million this year, about one third of one percent of the twenty odd billion given to bail out Anglo Irish Bank. And much government funding for the arts goes towards projects which are anything but elitist, such as the painting classes for older long-stay patients at Merlin Park Hospital or the popular creative writing classes provided for people with disabilities in Galway by the Brothers of Charity's Away with Words project. Such projects, and there are many others, bring colour and joy to the lives of those for whom such things are a crying need and no sort of luxury.

It is true that sometimes a cutback in a grant can provide an arts organisation with a necessary jolt; it is undeniable, for example, that the Irish Writers Centre in Dublin's Parnell Square is a livelier place now, more engaged with the broad writing community, than it was before its large annual grant was cut to nothing in 2009. But that is something of an exception. Most arts organisations perform miracles in terms of the amount they do with what is, in the grand scheme, very little money. Only the clinically insane get involved in the arts with financial gain in mind. The question for most in the sector has been and remains: how do we protect what we love to do from the ongoing economic carnage? This despite the fact that much of the time our one certain reward, even in the good times, is no security at all.

One of the main lines of argument which has been used by the National Campaign for the Arts and others as they've lobbied to try and limit the cutbacks has been that the arts have the potential to play an important role in a hoped-for economic recovery. It has even been said that Ireland's cultural image—everything from *Riverdance* to the reality of Ireland's position as a literary superpower—can play a role in attracting multinational investment. This is a very difficult argument for the left. But dismissing it out of hand gets us nowhere. It is a reflection of the fact that most Irish artists do not, as things stand, believe that there is any credible alternative to capitalism. Despite Seánie Fitzpatrick et al, the arguments put forward by the parties of the organised far left are seen by most to be only a little more believable than the predictions of mediums at Knock. Artists and poets and the like may have a reputation for not being in touch with what taxi drivers call 'the real world'. But being an artist of any sort is a difficult, if at times also very rewarding life, and most have learned to be ruthlessly practical in terms of where tomorrow's lunch is coming from. Promises of socialist castles in the air might appeal to some of the young, newly unemployed now hit with welfare cuts, but despite the van Gogh stereotype most artists are only interested in things that have a chance of actually happening.

The other problem for the left is that this campaign, using what most of the comrades would no doubt see as pro-capitalist arguments, has to date been pretty successful. The most miserable man in Ireland, Colm McCarthy, recommended in his Bord Snip Nua report that both Culture Ireland and the Irish Film Board be abolished. Both have to date avoided the axe—although there have been reductions in their budgets, as well as that of the Arts Council, which is by far the most important source of funding for artists and arts organisations of every stripe. The appointment by the government of Gabriel Byrne as our 'cultural ambassador' was an important success for the campaign in that it now makes it much more difficult for said same government to abolish Culture Ireland. If Irish artists aren't enabled to travel abroad to promote their work, then what precisely would be the point of having the man who once rolled in the hay with Maggie in *The Riordans* as our cultural ambassador?

The National Campaign for the Arts has fought its corner, using every pragmatic argument available to it. It deserves our support and any constructive suggestions the left might have. There is some concern that arguments about Ireland's cultural image being advantageous, when it comes to attracting inward investment, commodify the arts and might potentially turn our writers and actors and visual artists into court jesters paid to pleasure visitors from the boardrooms of global capitalism. I have to say that, to date, I have never seen a single instance where a funding agency tried to coax or pressurise an artist into following any sort of pro-business line in his or her work. The day an arts administrator tells me that I can't say this or that in a poem, I will resist as absolutely as I have already had to do when some of the more jaded hacks of the far left have on occasion tried to bully or jostle me into following their every line. But I don't think it's about to happen.

The pragmatism of the National Campaign for the Arts may sound like something from a very different world to the one inhabited by the large crowd who attended the livewire poetry and music event at the International Bar which I mentioned at the outset. And it is. At such events one is witnessing the new culture of post-Tiger Ireland being born, whereas the established arts organisations in most cases represent the cultural life that was during the years of endless honey. The new culture will continue to be driven forward by the whip of the recession. There are very hopeful signs that, come what may, artists will continue to make their art and work with others to find their audience.

In my own field, I was delighted of late to see that a group of emerging writers have come together to launch a new magazine, *The Poetry Bus*, despite having received no funding at all. Another young writer recently launched the fine online magazine *Wordlegs.com*. I was disappointed when the editor dropped her original rule that she would not accept submissions from writers over thirty years of age. It seemed to me a marvellously direct way of saying to the world: Here is the new generation, carving out its own space. The fogeys of yesteryear need not apply. That said, I did send her some poems recently: I refer you to my previous comment about artists having to be ruthlessly practical.

There has also been a significant flowering of new theatre

companies doing some interesting things. Fledgling theatre companies usually rely on a group of enthusiastic young people with time on their hands. These days there is no shortage of such young people looking for some place to put their talent and enthusiasm. I recently saw an excellent play, *The Quare Land*, staged as part of Galway Arts Festival by Decadent Theatre Company. It went right for the meat of our current crisis with wit and passion and managed also to be a great afternoon's entertainment.

The economic hell into which we have now descended will no doubt result in some arts organisations going under. Those who have got used to relying on large grants will find themselves facing out into a mean looking sea for the foreseeable. But some of the new publications and events I've mentioned will grow up to achieve real significance. From these will come the writers whose novels and short stories and poems will tell people fifty or a hundred years from now what it was like to be here today living in a country brought low by the wild gambling of our now fallen Great Gatsbys whose ghosts must surely have wandered the corridors of the G Hotel during this year's Galway Races.

It would be a very bad thing indeed if a new generation of writers and artists were to end up having to live on the slices of cold toast which were the staple diet of Patrick Kavanagh and Flann O'Brien. In the long run, there is nothing pretty about that sort of poverty. It tends, ultimately, to kill creativity. To play its role in making sure such an outcome does not fall on the heads of these writers and artists as yet unknown, it's important the left supports the National Campaign for the Arts. The arts are just as important in their way as the health service, education or social welfare. Even in these worst of times, there has to be more to life than hospital trolleys, damp school buildings and not enough dole. Any socialist who doesn't know this and act accordingly is no socialist worth being.

Red Banner magazine, September 2010

mainstream love hotel

by TODD SWIFT

I have to confess the line that kept coming to mind as I contemplated this review is not from any of Todd Swift's fine poems nor indeed from any other piece of poetic writing, but from that questionable 1980s duet by Elaine Paige and Barbara Dickson: *I Know Him So Well*. I have reviewed two of Todd's previous collections and wrote the introduction for his new and selected, *Seaway*, published by Salmon Poetry in 2008 and launched in London the night Barack Obama was elected President. I have never had any difficulty writing honest reviews, and have the gunshot wounds to prove it; but I know Todd and his work so well that there is a serious danger I could just end up repeating myself. My wife, Susan, assures me that I am excellent at repeating myself. Having allowed this reservation its moment, I was delighted at the opportunity to dive into Todd's latest offering, which is, if I have it right, his sixth full collection of poetry. Swift is a prolific poet indeed, not one of those to wander Larkin's nut-strewn roads moaning about the latest bout of poetic constipation. He is someone for whom the whole world is, in some sense, a poem waiting to be written. And every subject will have its day.

Todd is at his best when he allows himself to be his own subject. A major issue for him in recent years, as anyone who follows his *Eyewear* blog will know, is religious faith and the difficulties there of. One of the best poems in *mainstream love hotel*, 'New Theology', deals with precisely this issue:

> Here is the god not believed in, and here,
> broken, as rain is set apart, unmade

is the way a bed never slept in is calm
when deep within it is a radiant pain.

The poem's eleven couplets are full of fine original imagery, and it is the sort of poem that may not convert Richard Dawkins, but will give many an agnostic pause.

Even beyond the issue of belief or disbelief, there is beauty in someone taking their own faith seriously enough to write about it well. These days the worlds of religion and fringe politics—all the way from the Irish Catholic Church through the endless smiles of New Ageism to the nonsense of anti-war protestors from Shropshire and the like converting to Islam—sometimes seem to be populated entirely by people who couldn't string a sentence together if their lives depended on it, which they perhaps should. Not that secularists are immune to the idea that certainty gives the believer in said certainties the permission to stop thinking, which is the root of most bad writing; the back issues of *Socialist Worker* are living (or should that be dying?) proof of this. Swift has one important thing in common with Christopher Hitchens—a man he would likely disagree with on almost any issue—whatever you may think of his beliefs, you have to admit he writes very well about them.

The Todd Swift I know has always had a healthy dose of perversity in his soul. *mainstream love hotel* confirms this is still alive and 'gyrating', if not exactly healthy. 'The talking cure' is an excellent example of the decadent fantasy poem, with the strange ring of truth to it, which Swift does so well. It is a poem Roddy Lumsden could have written in one of his kinkier moments:

You cut your hair very short exactly three hours after
I told you how much I liked your hair long. Bold.
Bad baby. But the pageboy cut works…

'The afternoon drinkers' is another strong poem about the loneliness of the long distance drinker, those who serve their time 'glass by yellow glass' and for whom 'the jukebox [is] the only nightingale'. This reeks of downbeat English decadence. It is as if the Soho inhabited by Dylan Thomas and Francis Bacon had been described by Philip Larkin on a dark day. The poem also combines inventive use of religious imagery: 'the tray of ash // the only convent for a sacred heart' with words you'd never hear in church: 'the arse and tits of car posters'. This is perhaps what Todd does best. One sometimes gets the impression that his politer lyrics are a kind of trick on the reader which gives him the element of surprise when he decides to unveil the spoiled priest in a brothel (or some other such enemy of politeness and hope) he has waiting around the corner for us.

Swift is a poet permanently engaged with the news; almost every world event of any note—from the death of Michael Foot to the Winter Olympics in Vancouver—could typically be the subject of comment on his blog. In 'Love song in a time of inflation' and 'Light Sweet Crude' he makes unlikely poetry from the language of financial 'futures' and 'securitisation'. Swift is to some extent a pop poet in the way that Frank O'Hara was, although Swift's mood tends to be darker. He is a great namedropper of pop culture artefacts, as likely to reference *Elle* magazine, or the Cocteau Twins or Radiohead, or *Astral Weeks* or *Moon River*—all of which achieve mention in *mainstream love hotel*—as he is to mention Pan, Bacchus and Aquitaine, who also appear in the collection. Reading Swift's poetry can sometimes be like biting into a rich chocolate cake, some of the ingredients of which are mildly hallucinogenic. His poems are places where anything can happen, and often does.

mainstream love hotel is a fine snapshot of a poet-in-transition, as Swift continues to shake himself free of his too-many-to-mention influences and becomes more and more his own poet. Ultimately, he is at his best when he is at the centre of his own poems and all inessential elements have been stripped away. I was particularly struck by the powerful 'These Days', a poem in which Swift reflects on his changing aspirations in middle age. In 'The Life with a Hole in it' Larkin wrote about the "Three-handed struggle between / Your wants, the world's for you, and (worse) / The unbeatable slow machine / That brings you what you'll get." Swift has an altogether more stoical, almost Zen, take on the way life tends to make mincemeat of our more lofty ambitions:

I'd thought to have my work
done by now, to have reached

the goals set out long ago,
I won't get there now
no need to, here, see
what was earned, not owed,
these days of you and me—
more than pensions, savings,
toil, long hours, ever bring—
says beginning with us in bed

and ending with us asleep—
between is the time worked
on, to make, and keep
no other days
no other ways
these are them, here,
in the basket, glinting like coins,
fish fresh and shining from the sea.

Where Larkin would surely have found some way of making the
reader want to reach for the sleeping pills and razor blades, the
closing image here affirms life as it is actually lived in a way that
Heaney would surely approve of. Swift is a poet unafraid to give
both darkness and light a fair, fighting chance. This makes the
project I know he's working on now, a collection of devastating
confessional lyrics in the manner of the great Americans—Lowell,
Berryman and Delmore Schwartz—a very exciting prospect
indeed. Todd Swift is a big poet and a dramatic character always on
the lookout for the next heroic idea at a time when we are short
of next heroic ideas. It is precisely this jarring relationship with his
environment which gives Todd his essential originality as a poet.

The Wolf magazine, Summer 2010

Poetry, politics and the left

An interview with Kevin Higgins conducted by Aindrias
Ó'Cathasaigh

*Much of your poetry deals with overtly political subject matter, so you
obviously don't subscribe to the view that 'poetry and politics don't mix'.
Does that view persist, or is there a level of openness to political poetry in
Ireland today?*
I think there is no small amount of confusion on this issue. It
would be fair to say that most poets, most readers of contemporary
poetry, and the majority of those who attend readings have a vague
idea that the role of poetry is to question and oppose things as they
are, rather than to support the status quo. In the majority of cases,
this tends to amount to little more than the requisite poem or two
about Palestine or the Iraq war in collections that are mostly made
up of what has been uncharitably called the poetry of personal
anecdote. This is a huge generalisation, of course, and as with any
such generalisation, is more than a little unfair to many. There are
a minority of recently emerged poets for whom poetry and radical
left wing politics of one variety or another are inseparable. In a
word, yes, there is openness to political poetry in Ireland today.
Whatever you have to say on whatever subject, as long as it's well
said, people will listen, and the poems will make their way out into
the world and find a readership.

*So if poetry is open to politics, is politics open to poetry? Do you think
there is a recognition among left-wing activists that poetry has a meaningful
role to play in the socialist project?*
If by left-wing activists you mean those who are involved in
organisations proposing a transformation more radical than
installing Éamon Gilmore as Tánaiste or Mary Lou McDonald as

Junior Minister for Nothing-in-Particular, I'd have to say that the answer would be more No than Yes. Certainly there are those active on the left who have a real appreciation of poetry and the arts in general, and some recognition of the role that poetry can play in sharpening one's understanding of the world as it is now, has been and will come to be. But these tend to be people who are either on their way out of active involvement, certainly in terms of being members of organised groups and parties, or are in some sense dissidents within these parties.

The organised far left is, as I have learned from bitter experience, still pretty much addicted to the idea that poetry is only of use when it has an obvious and immediate propaganda value in the campaign of the moment. They view with suspicion people who think for themselves and also tend to see activities such as writing poetry as a diversion from the 'struggle'. I would have been pretty bad on these issues myself back in my workerist days, so I do cut them some slack. But my work teaching poetry workshops and creative writing classes has really brought home to me that any attempt to force on a poet an agenda with which he or she isn't imaginatively engaged does more than diminish the poetry. In the end it destroys it. The only real role the organised far left seems to see for poetry is the usual one or two suspects reading a poem at the end of the demo type of thing. Culture isn't a peripheral thing: it is central. And anyone who wants to control the arts for narrow political ends would do very bad things indeed if they ever came to power.

Surely there will always be some kind of tension between political activists trying to offer straightforward answers to political issues on the one hand, and poets trying to explore ambiguities in life's nooks and crannies on the other? Is it not necessary—or even creative—for those imperatives to clash from time to time?

I agree that such a clash could potentially be very creative. There will be tensions between those primarily involved in writing political statements and those involved in writing poems. They are very different activities. Writing a political manifesto or a leaflet necessarily moves one in the direction of simplifying the issues rather than going into the complexities. Also, a leaflet is not the opinion of one person but of a group, and would obviously be very different to, say, a poem or short story, which if it is to be any good must necessarily be the independent creation of one person's imagination. But that's not the issue here. The real problem is that most of the organised far left groups run their internal affairs in a very cultish way—small groups of people endlessly engaged in convincing themselves that they are absolutely right and everyone else absolutely wrong—with the result that many of their members, and I'd say their entire leaderships, have no use for anything that doesn't further the building of the party. For them culture is not a separate zone in which what you describe as "life's nooks and crannies" can be creatively explored, ambiguities and all. For them culture has no role at all other than to confirm the points of view they already hold dear. It is a given that when there is an immediate public issue on which a leaflet or press release needs to be written or a speech has to be made, straightforwardness is to be favoured every time over ambiguity. But a society without the ability to question and criticise itself, which is precisely what the best poems and plays and films do, is a profoundly dysfunctional society. And even small left wing groups are their own kind of society.

So is the problem here not so much that the left suffers from bad cultural politics, but that it suffers from bad politics, full stop?
I think that the bad cultural politics is important, because it gives us a taste of the type of regime the organised far left would impose were it to come to power. For example, I doubt we'd be having this conversation in such a public and open way if the people in question were ensconced in government buildings. The way the organised far left deals with internal issues is cavalier in the extreme. They don't even abide by their own stated rules half the time, and there is a huge amount of cynicism in the way that people are dealt with: again and again, people who have given these organisations decades of their lives are just tossed aside. The internal regimes of the far left organisations are inherently undemocratic, hence the constant splits and denunciations of former members. I've even heard of people being expelled by text message! I've known too many cases involving too many people over far too long a period of time to believe that this is anything other than a systematic failure, rather than the result of the shortcomings of this or that individual or group of individuals. This next statement will no doubt cause steam to start emerging from some comrades' ears, but it seems to me obvious that Fianna Fáil, Fine Gael and the Labour Party are infinitely more democratic

organisations than any of those on the organised far left. They can tolerate internal dissent in a way that the far left cannot, and that is a great strength.

The cultural issue leads straight to the democracy issue, which in turn leads right to the disaster that was the aftermath of the Russian revolution. What Russia proved is that, without the active participation of the majority of the people in the decision-making processes, socialism cannot work. If you're going to abolish the market, which at least tells you something about what people want, albeit in a very distorted and anarchic way, you must allow people the freedom to tell you what they want and how they want it. Otherwise socialist planning is entirely impractical.

I know I'm not the first to say this, but it is obvious now that the beliefs (1) that socialism is in some sense historically inevitable, (2) that it will solve all of the world's problems, and (3) that it can only be brought about by a tightly organised group which does not tolerate public dissent from the party line, will always lead to disaster and probably to the restoration of capitalism as happened in Russia and eastern Europe. After all, if you believe you have all the answers to the world's problems and can create a heaven on earth, then it is possible to justify any number of lies, any number of purges of deviant petit-bourgeois elements to achieve such an end. Trotsky and Lenin and Rosa Luxemburg and Co. did not have at their disposal the information we now do. They did not know that the limits placed on internal dissent and free expression generally in what was a time of civil war in Russia, far from being a bulwark against the restoration of capitalism, would turn out to be the first step in the long journey back towards capitalism. And I've no doubt that Marx would run screaming in the opposite direction from most of those who today claim to be his followers. Saying this sort of thing causes me something close to physical pain. I don't want it to be true. Over a period of many years I have tried every other way of looking at it. But I can no longer avoid the obvious which has stared me in the face every day for at least the past five or six years.

Some people reading comments like this from you, and even some of your poetry, will conclude that here is a disillusioned former socialist who has turned renegade. You obviously reject the organised far left as it is currently—but are you rejecting revolutionary socialism as a political philosophy too?

I know there are many who'll react to what I'm saying in the way you describe. In the past, I would have taken that line myself. Now I tend to view that as one of the ways the far left dodges valid questions: instead of bothering to come up with a proper answer, they attack the questioner. To put it at its bluntest: even if I am now in the pay of Dick Cheney and the Israelis and Galway Chamber of Commerce, that doesn't absolve them from having to answer the points I'm making. The organised far left are meant to be the vanguard of the international working class, the most advanced and forward-looking people in the world. So come on, boys and girls, step up to the plate and demolish my argument.

I am in favour of all of the things that revolutionary socialists pretend to be in favour of. Refusing to stay quiet about flagrant hypocrisy on the left certainly has nothing at all to do with "rejecting revolutionary socialism". What I really think is that if there is to be any hope at all of a better and workable and democratic version of socialism, then the far left needs to undergo a complete reformation, and to this end its nose has to be rubbed in all its worst mistakes. A society in which all the vast resources of the planet were under the democratic control of the man and woman in the street would be infinitely better than what we have now. The fear, the insecurity which is affecting almost everyone you meet at the moment is truly awful. A truly democratic socialist plan implemented on a global scale would have to be better than this. However, no one, and I include myself in that, will be convinced to support, or even to tolerate, a system in which there is a one party dictatorship and the whole country is run like a big fat FÁS scheme gone mad. We will not go gently into that good night, because that would be much worse than what we have—yes, worse than NAMA and Brian Cowen. But saying no to all the prospective Dear Leaders doesn't in my mind amount to "rejecting revolutionary socialism".

If we can focus on a specific example, 'Firewood', a poem in your last collection. Some people believe you were advocating military intervention in Darfur under cover of the UN, or at least tacitly supporting the idea. Where do you stand on that issue?
I don't think that people who read this poem as me "advocating military intervention" really understand what poems are and how they are born. For a while I had been of the view that sections of the left had been accommodating themselves to Islam in a way that

is not at all socialist. Obviously, one has to oppose any type of religious discrimination against any group, and I always will, but the use of the slogan "We are all Hezbollah now!" during the Israeli attack on Lebanon in 2006 was not good. Sections of the left seemed all too willing to act like cheerleaders for what remains an Islamic fundamentalist group—with no offence at all intended to actual cheerleaders, most of whom have never committed such serious political mistakes. Anyway, when I read the article which contained the fatal few words "It's problematic to describe this as genocide" something snapped in me, which is the way a poem is usually born. I saw that article as amounting to a kind of apology for the Sudanese government and the Janjaweed. The glibness of the language seemed to indicate a wish that the difficult issue of what has been happening in Darfur would go away so that the writer could go back to his preferred subject: George W Bush and the wars in Iraq and Afghanistan. I know that the situation in the Sudan is horribly complicated, with Muslims massacring other Muslims and so on, and that there are no easy solutions, but the Sudanese government and the Janjaweed are clearly the bad guys, and this article was trying to muddy the waters. When you come across a phrase as glib as "It's problematic to describe this as genocide", dodgy politics is never far behind. To me, this was a section of the organised far left just shrugging its shoulders about a conflict that had seen the government-sponsored murder of tens of thousands and the displacement of many hundreds of thousands. I have no answers in relation to Darfur: the poem is not about that. I don't think a UN-sponsored invasion would make things better, but I would not actively oppose such action if I thought it was the least worst option. I understand the left's desire to maintain its independent political position on these issues and to offer its own uniquely socialist answer, which obviously has no role for the UN or liberal interventionism of the type that took place in Kosovo. However, I have no time at all for the meaningless sloganeering that often goes on in these situations: the appeals to the phantom armies of the Bosnian and Rwandan working classes which were the response of some left groups to those situations. If you have no real answer, then far better to admit that rather than trying to bullshit your way to a unified theory of everything. The writer of that article had nothing to say about Darfur, and he missed an excellent opportunity to say it. Every possible pressure should be put on the Sudanese government in relation to what it's been doing in Darfur. And the effect of that article, if it had any effect at all, would have been to take the pressure off. It amounted to scabbing on the people of Darfur in their hour of great need: that's what provoked the poem.

The rapid move from economic boom to bust has shaken a lot of certainties in Irish society, and opened up space for questioning and for potential alternatives. What role do you see for writers and artists in that process?
Last year I used a few pages from The Great Gatsby, the scene in which the narrator describes the night he first went to one of Gatsby's lavish gatherings at his mansion, as the basis for a writing exercise. Lehman Brothers had filed for bankruptcy the day that course began. I always give the historical context when I'm introducing a piece of writing to students, and mostly it seems to float over their heads. This time when I said that what was being described in this book, the jazz age of the 1920s, was an era very similar to the one which had just died a very sudden death here in Ireland, for the first time since I started teaching writing, I got a real sense that what was happening outside—in what Marxists like to call 'the real world'—was in the room with us and influencing how we talked, not just about the literature of the past, but also the stories and poems the students were writing themselves. That is a big change and will I'm sure in the long run, or perhaps even in the short run, change Irish writing. My own guess would be that there'll be a lot of novels taking to task the Celtic Tiger era in the next couple of years. Now it's over, the boom era is somehow more digestible.

Also, though, there may be less outlets for new writers. Certainly publishers will take less risks and the arts sector in general will have less funding. I think that if the grassroots literary events which have grown so dramatically in the past few years all manage to keep going, and the signs are that they will, then they'll become forums where the tangible discontent and anger that's out there about what has happened and is going to happen will be given literary expression. This will especially be the case if we don't see emigration starting up again in a serious way, as it did during the 1980s. Either way, things will not be as they have been. There was a brashness about the Irish literary scene before last year which fed into some of the writing, an idea that crisis was something you only saw on *Reeling in The Years*, that had nothing to do with where we thought we were. I think there will likely, as time goes on, be new literary magazines which reflect the turn world events have taken. This happened during the 1930s when magazines such as *The Partisan Review* became very important. There is a crying need for new literary magazines run by younger writers with a fresh way of looking at things. No one will, nor should, listen to the rants and gibes of cranky old literary gents who've never got over the fact that Neil Jordan and Paul Durcan are more successful than they are. But I would be most interested to read the reflections and rants of writers in their twenties, the new generation who will eventually put me in the old peoples' home.

In terms of what role writers should play, I don't think a writer can be judged by the number of demos he or she goes on or the number of angry letters he or she writes to *The Irish Times*. These things may make the person in question an excellent activist, but tell us very little about their writing. The writers I am always interested in are those who see everything in the world as their subject, and ruthlessly write the truth as they see it, come what may. Far better to do this than become a yes man or woman for this or that popular front.

Red Banner magazine, December 2009

Dancing On Prospect Hill
As Hard Times Come Again

In the Autumn of 2007 Margaret Flannery of Galway University Hospitals Arts Trust phoned to ask if I'd become the organisation's Writer In Residence. As poets generally do, unless the person doing the asking is Charles Manson or Osama Bin Laden, I said yes. We self-employed poets go about our business in fear of the day the phone stops ringing and we are left alone with our line breaks. The residency, Margaret explained, would not involve creative writing but some serious creative listening. The Hospitals Arts Trust produces an annual publication in which the true life stories of long-stay patients at Units 5 and 6 of Merlin Park Hospital are compiled using reminiscence techniques. Armed with my dictaphone, I would meet patients once a week for an hour long session in the day room.

Each year's publication is themed. Topics previously covered have included school days and the environment. The theme for 2007/8 would, we decided, be entertainment. Many of the patients are in their eighties and nineties. So they well remember Ireland as it was before the advent of RTE Television on New Year's Eve, 1961 and have witnessed unimaginable changes during their lifetimes. Each Monday afternoon we visited them we were inevitably greeted by the tinkling sound of the theme for *Eastenders* wafting out from the dayroom. Our first task was to discreetly turn the television down and gather a group of the interested and the talkative around the table.

There is nothing like a hospital day room on a Monday afternoon to make one suddenly aware of one's mortality. Shakespeare had a point: the sound and fury with which we fill our lives, and the lives of others, really does in the end signify not very much. This realisation was made all the more acute for me by the fact that, when I was just ten years old, my own mother almost died of Hodgkin's Disease in the same hospital. I remember us leaving her back there on December 26th, 1977. The memory of her at the doorway as we drove away is a picture that never fades. Merlin Park was originally built as a TB hospital and is arranged in a series of small units surrounded by tall green trees on the very edge of Galway City. On a July day when everything is on the up, its surroundings give it something approaching beauty. But on a wet February day the huge unloved chimney stack glowering in the distance can make it rather resemble a concentration camp.

It became for me the place where the poetry world ended and things got absolutely real. Having met many poets over these past few years, I know that most are absolutely decent, but that there are those who'd cut your throat to get half a haiku into the Moycullen News. I exaggerate, absolutely. But the desperate egos all too common in our world are nowhere to be found in the dayrooms of Units Five and Six.

The great thing about this project is that it's not about me, but people like Ellen Melody, Mary Kennedy, Madeleine Moloney and Louis Hanley. Ellen told me her memories of people entertaining themselves by drinking Poitín and listening to that well known Galway man, Lord Haw Haw, on the radio. Mary Kennedy remembered the dances which used to take place on Prospect Hill, where she grew up; and so the title of our 2008 publication became *The Cat's Cradle Volume 3—Dancing on Prospect Hill*. Louis Hanley told of his time working as a projectionist "helping this man who…used to hire out halls to show films. In the summer time he had his own marquee. It was terrific, great entertainment. It used to be packed…We'd have films that were ahead of Galway even…until the crowds dwindled as the television took over." Louis also told me about the time he saw John Steinbeck with John Huston in *Paddy Burke's* pub in Clarinbridge and that he regrets to this day not going over to talk to him. Madeleine Moloney kept me up to date with the latest from *Fair City* and also gave me regular updates on the race between Barack Obama and Hillary Clinton.

In this year's publication, *The Cat's Cradle Volume 4—Hard Times Come Again*, we went right for the huge topic of the moment. I knew that the patients would have plenty of experience of hard times past against which to compare what we're going through now. We began our weekly sessions last September and as the sessions went by the news just kept getting worse…Lehman

Brothers went belly up, and Anglo Irish was nationalised as Kathleen Moloney told me how in the old days: "people would go to the shop. The shop would give them the goods to feed themselves and they would pay later when they'd sell an animal...It would happen many times that they wouldn't pay it back." It is perhaps only the extent of the 'paying later' which has changed! In our final session Louis Hanley came up with a possible solution to our current woes, which sounded to me almost like a page from a Joe Higgins election manifesto. Louis suggested that the wealthiest people in the country who have "taken a big hit lately, but... still have a lot" should be asked to cough up something in the region of "€20 billion...to help the country back on its feet." Louis says that he is available should either of the beleaguered Brians wish to contact him regarding his suggested solution.

Since 2007 I've met some hugely inspiring people in Units 5 and 6. Listening to Florie Lydon talk about the job she had rescuing people from under the rubble during the Blitz reminded me that there are bigger worries than the latest award you didn't win or possible reductions in Arts Council grants. And for that I am eternally gratefully to her.

Poetry Ireland Newsletter, July–August 2009

The Cat's Cradle volume 3: Dancing on Prospect Hill (2008) & *The Cat's Cradle volume 4: Hard Times Come Again* (2009) were both launched at the respective years' Cúirt Festivals in Galway.

Love, Sex and the Revolution

Calling the Tune by MAUREEN GALLAGHER

I first met Maureen Gallagher in the summer of 1985 on a protest outside Dunnes Stores' Terryland branch in support of the workers at the Henry Street branch, Dublin who were on strike because one of them had been sacked for refusing to handle South African goods. Maureen has been an activist and member of a small Trotskyist group for almost three decades now. The poems in *Calling The Tune* divide into three general categories: political poems, love poems and erotic poems. Her political poems cover everything from clerical sexual abuse—'December Rain' and 'Shrouding A Crime'—and the now apparently dead parrot of the Salthill Airshow—'The Airshow'—to our current rather unpleasant economic situation—'Subprime': "the man climbs into a bin on a cold night / in September, the month of late strawberries / and blueberries from the US where subprime / lending pulls banks down around its ankles / and the wealthy psychologist bleats on air / to please not worry about nursing homes / or alienating sons who fear they'll be left / to pick up the tab if Northern Rock / goes belly-up like the homeless man…" Now, it is undeniably true that the far left have spent decades dreaming of the sort of 'crisis of capitalism' we are currently going through; it is all Joe Higgins's fantasies come true. Maureen's book was published in December and even these few months later the "if" in "if Northern Rock / goes belly-up" is a word from a lost golden age. There are no such 'ifs' anymore. My one big quibble with Maureen's poetry is that, when writing about politics, the irony that is generally her trademark tends to give way to a 'we are right and that's the end of it' tone reminiscent of the political speeches of Vanessa Redgrave. Irony is the best possible insurance policy against the totalitarianism which is still rampant on the far left. To be blunt, despite everything, give me Seanie Fitzpatrick any day, if the only alternative is a one party dictatorship led by someone like Kevin McLoughlin, the real leader of the Socialist Party for which genial Joe Higgins is a mere front man, or Kieran Allen, chief guru and hatchet wielder of the Socialist Workers Party.

The poems in which Maureen faces the vicissitudes of love going wrong are much stronger. 'No Strings' is up there with the best work of Carol Ann Duffy: "I encouraged you / to write your / own world. // You did that / but ended up with / more characters / than space. // So you cut me down from chapter / to paragraph / to sentence / to full / stop. // Then being modern, / you dispensed with / punctuation / altogether". And Maureen's two eating-as-sex poems, 'There's A Peach In The Fridge' and 'On The Subject Of Eating Cake Creatively' are perfect satires on the sexual incompatibility of men and woman. The voice in both poems is the sort one might expect to hear in an instructional video and the effect is hilarious.

Galway Advertiser, March 2009

All Poetry's Children Under
The One Wide Roof

Over The Edge provides a platform where emerging writers, both poets and fiction writers, can read their work to a decent sized, appreciative audience. It was born in Galway City Library on Wednesday, January 22nd, 2003, when the first Over The Edge: Open Reading took place. The featured readers on that innocent Wednesday evening were poets Maureen Gallagher and Caoilinn Hughes and fiction writer Jim Mullarkey. The featured readers each read for fifteen minutes and after they'd finished there was an open-mic at which members of the audience could read a poem or short extract from a story or novel they were working on. My good wife, Susan Millar DuMars, was the MC for the evening. And that has remained the format ever since.

We guarantee new writers an audience to try their work out on. Our smallest crowd over the past six years has been twenty five, our largest around ninety. The average of late has been about fifty. And it is not all the same worn crowd turning up month after month. Different readers will draw different crowds. Our e-mail list, the key to the promotion of our readings, now runs to several thousand. At this stage, a decent percentage of the population of Galway City have attended at least one Over The Edge reading. One of the questions I always ask myself when we are lining up the featured readers for any given month is: what niche audience will each of them bring along? For example, which writers' groups are they members of?

One of the featured readers at the sixth anniversary Over The Edge reading in ten days time is Áine Tierney, a fiction writer who now lives back in her home county of Tipperary, but who did the MA in Writing at NUIG some years back and used to work in our local Post Office. As I write Newcastle Post Office is awash with posters for the reading and Áine's former workmates are all planning to come. One of the other readers is well known poet Tom French, who studied at NUI Galway and so is well known in these parts. My friend Gary King thinks my experience of tiny left wing meetings, during my long years as a member of the Militant Tendency, has filled me with a chronic fear of small crowds. He perhaps has a point. Since I turned forty I have less tolerance for many things, and none at all for the idea that it's impossible to get decent turnouts at poetry readings. If you have a positive attitude, an inclusive approach and, most important of all, you persist, then your audience will grow.

That word 'inclusive' is much abused by politicians and poverty industry professionals in search of votes and grants. What it means in this context is not that all poems or all poets are equal. To paraphrase George Orwell: some poems, some poets are far more equal than others. To deny that leads us towards the absurdity of pretending that, say, Shakespeare is no better nor worse a poet than those fledging male poets whose only outlet to date has been to scribble their masterpieces on the walls of public conveniences around Galway City. It's not that I haven't, from time to time, seen some snappy lines scrawled in such places. But, all things considered, Shakespeare is better. However, if one of Galway's toilet wall poets wants to come along and read at the open-mic, he would be very welcome. All must have an audience, if not necessarily prizes.

To properly understand the role Over The Edge plays it's necessary to see it in the context of the multiplicity of rigorous literary workshops which take place around Galway City at Galway Arts Centre, at Galway Technical Institute, at GMIT, on the MA in Writing at NUIG and elsewhere. In any given month the majority of those who read at the open-mic are participants in one creative writing class or another. It is rarely a case of the wild unedited jottings of some Edgar Allan Poe in the making being given a histrionic airing (although that does occasionally happen) and far more often a case of poems in which a great deal of time, thought and consideration has been invested being given their first public hearing.

We use the open-mic as an unofficial audition for featured reader spots. Our job as events organisers and workshop facilitators (at last count we were facilitating ten writing workshops a week between us) is not to make everyone a famous poet. Even if it were desirable, not everyone who puts words on paper is aiming for

Faber & Faber and the Nobel Prize. For some, just getting their words down in the best way they can is what it's all about. They have other lives to attend to. That said, many of those who began at our open-mic have gone on to be featured readers, to achieve publication and win major prizes.

In 2008 alone Mary Madec won the Hennessy Award for Poetry; Lorna Shaughnessy had her first collection, *Torching The Brown River*, published by Salmon Poetry; and Miceál Kearney had his debut collection, *Inheritance*, published by Doire Press on foot of his victory in the North Beach Poetry Grand Slam. The next year or so will see the publication of first collections by three other Over The Edge alumni, Aideen Henry, John Corless and Celeste Augé, all by Salmon Poetry.

I first met Lorna Shaughnessy when she phoned me in October 2003 to say she had been writing poems "on the quiet" for a number of years and wanted someone to have a look at them. She was a featured reader at the December 2003 reading and also read the first Cúirt/Over The Edge showcase reading in April 2006. A poem from Lorna's collection was included in this year's *Forward Book of Poetry*. Her days of doing it "on the quiet" are over.

When I first met Miceál Kearney he'd just started a Creative Writing for Beginners course at GMIT, facilitated by Susan, and was extremely nervous and monosyllabic. I was putting out chairs for the September 2005 Over The Edge: Open Reading and he asked me to put his name down for the open-mic. Since then he has won the Cúirt Festival Poetry Grand Slam, The Baffle Festival prize, the Cúisle Festival Poetry Slam to name just a few; his work has appeared in journals such as *The Shop*, *Orbis* and *Envoi*; and he has read his work in Chicago, Brighton and Slovenia. These days, Miceál is a little less monosyllabic.

Perhaps the best example of what I'm talking about, though, was Mary Madec winning the 2008 Hennessy Award for Poetry. The Hennessy Award ceremony took place the week the Cúirt Festival was happening here. Mary had been selected to read at the now annual Cúirt/Over The Edge showcase reading. Each year we make a shortlist of those writers who've read for us and don't yet have a book published. The poets are then asked to submit three poems each which we pass on the Cúirt committee, who choose the four or five writers to be showcased that particular year. It's a huge step forward for a bookless new writer to make it onto the programme of a festival such as Cúirt alongside the likes of Seamus

Heaney, Nikki Giovanni & Edna O'Brien. And it's not at all tokenistic, but always rigorously competitive. We can never guess which of the short-listed writers will be chosen. Anyway, last year Mary won the Hennessy and came back to Galway like the conquering heroine she was and performed brilliantly to a large audience on the main Cúirt stage at the Town Hall Theatre. RTE Radio's *The Arts Show* recorded the reading and interviewed Mary afterwards. I first met Mary at a launch of Crannóg magazine in 2004. She was introduced to me as someone who "sometimes writes a few poems in her spare time." Since January 2005 Mary has been a valuable participant in the poetry workshops I facilitate at Galway Arts Centre. She sometimes writes poems while stuck in traffic jams. Nothing seems to stop her.

What makes Over The Edge work is the combination of openness and rigorous standards. If we think that you could hold your own reading for fifteen minutes alongside, say, Dennis O'Driscoll or Medbh McGuckian or Colette Bryce—to name just three of the established poets who've been featured readers at Over The Edge—then we will give you a chance. You might fly. Or you might fall a little flat. But either way, no one will have died. One of our unpublished featured readers once spoke for seven minutes before reading a word of poetry. Most such early reading failures can be put down to nerves. And it is far better to be plagued with nerves than plagued with ego. Nerves you'll learn to control. And there would be something wrong if you weren't a little nervous the first time you're asked to do a fifteen minute reading with an established poet on the bill beside you. The first time I read my work in public, at the Poets' Podium in Tralee in March 1997, I was suitably terrified. But if you're a beginner poet, an overdose of ego will be the end of you. It will make you see constructive criticism as personal slight. Others will listen to the available advice, improve their poems and move on ahead of you. And of course every success of theirs will hit you like a smack in the gob. They'll win the Patrick Kavanagh Award, the Hennessy, the Nobel. They'll be published by Faber and invited to read in Athens and Tokyo. You'll either give up. Or worse than that, you'll vanish down dark alleys and into whiskey bottles, consoling yourself with the fact that Kavanagh too was misunderstood in his day. I exaggerate, ever so slightly.

The final thing I'll say is that Over The Edge has no political agenda apart from making sure that every poet has his or her say and that, even if you disagree with what's been said, you listen. In

October 2006, one of the featured reader was Yvonne Green, a widely published poet based in London, who describes herself as an "observant Jew and a Zionist". To close her reading Yvonne read a poem which was basically an attack on Hezbollah for, the poem implied, starting the 2006 war with Israel. Yvonne then said that she would be open to comments from the audience. I remember thinking "Hmmm. Now this could get interesting!" At that I looked at the clock and it was touching 7.45pm, which meant that we had just fifteen minutes to complete the open mic; I am very much in favour of open-mics being time limited and not rambling on forever. But this was cutting it a bit fine. So, I went out to have a word with the librarians to let them know that we might run about five minutes over time; the library always closes at 8pm.

As I was on my way out Susan introduced the first open-mic reader. It was a young school teacher from County Galway, who opened by saying that, following Yvonne's reference to the recent Israel-Hezbollah war he was now going to read a different poem from the one he'd originally intended. His poem took the diametrically opposed pro-Palestinian view. I remember hearing the immortal line: "Did the Nazis teach you nothing?" as I exited the room and I was glad I was exiting. But everyone listened and no one interrupted, just as they had listened to Yvonne. Just as they listened to Gordon Hewitt, the Derry-based performance poet and Socialist Workers Party member, who got the audience, including my own mother, to participate in a sing song. At Over The Edge you'll find all poetry's children under the one wide roof. And that's as it should be.

Poetry: Reading It, Writing It, Publishing It (Salmon Poetry, 2009. Compiled and edited by Jessie Lendennie)

From the Yamana Indians to Desmond Fennell

The Given Note: Traditional Music and Irish Poetry
by SEÁN CROSSON

This substantial book began as part of Seán Crosson's research for his doctoral dissertation at the Centre for Irish Studies in NUIG. An idea central to it is that poetry is a kind of spoken music. Crosson refers to C.M. Bowra's study of the songs of the pre-literate Yamana Indians: ' "composed of ordinary sequences of apparently senseless syllables, without meaning in the language of the Yamana tribe or any other." For Bowra, such "senseless sounds" constitute "the most primitive kind of song. They anticipate later developments by making the human voice conform to a tune in a regular way, but the first step to poetry came when their place was taken by real words." Consequently, Bowra argues that poetry is "in its beginnings intimately welded with music".'

Crosson uses this method to contextualise the work of Irish poets such as Patrick Kavanagh, Nuala Ní Dhomhnaill, Cathal O'Searcaigh, Seamus Heaney, Ciaran Carson & Gearóid MacLochlainn. Of most interest to Crosson is poetry as public performance for a given community, a kind of poetry version of the traditional Irish music 'session'. The thrust of Crosson's argument appears to question the self-obsession of much lyric poetry, with its relentless overuse of the 'I' at the expense of the more community-minded 'we'. In chapter five Crosson seems to criticise Seamus Heaney. Although he leaves most of the talking to Desmond Fennell, who steps into the breach in the form of a quotation: "much of Heaney's poetry in the 70s could be regarded as private musing ... with any general views censored out...But

Heaney, with long Irish and English traditions of poetry as public speech behind him, had hesitated to commit himself to the 'private meditation' concept." Fennell argues that the praise of his "powerful champion", at Harvard, Professor Helen Vendler, was the final ruination of Heaney as a public poet: "the result can be noticed in the increased self-absorption and indifference to readers...he has been consciously not speaking to us, even to say nothing." Now, while it's undeniable that much contemporary lyric poetry, with its more than occasional obscurity and foregrounded 'I', is in serious danger of disappearing up its own rear end; there are dangers also in the Fennell argument, which is presented uncritically here.

It is one thing for a poet to speak to his or her community in poems. It is something else to ask that poet to follow a particular political line, which is, I think, what Fennell had in mind. Every community has lies it wants told. Sometimes, the poet's role is to face down the community and tell them truths they collectively refuse to admit. Without its audience poetry is nothing, Crosson's thesis is spot on there. But the individual voice must be defended, however oblique or inconvenient its message. Anyone who doubts this should remember that one of the firmest twentieth century advocates of accessible poems for the community was one Mr Josef Stalin. This is a hugely erudite book which answers many questions but raises others.

Galway Advertiser, January 2009

AZALEA—Journal of Korean Literature & Culture

(Volume One)

In one important respect we Irish have been lucky: the near genocide of our mid-nineteenth century famine and the sustained religious persecution our ancestors suffered were not the only gifts British rule gave us; colonisation also bequeathed us the English language. This has been hugely important in that it has made our North/South divide and recently ended Northern 'troubles' culturally sexy. This is especially obvious when one observes the way contemporary Irish poetry is typically received in those twin centres of the English language poetry world, New York and London. It is undeniably easier for an Irish poet to provoke interest in his or her work from academics, journals and publishers in those key centres, where things that matter happen, than is the case for a poet from Australia, New Zealand and, dare I say it, Canada. However wickedly an Irish poet may satirise all things Irish, the moment he or she steps up to a lectern on a US university campus, it's clear that what they are doing connects to an easily accessible tradition going back via Heaney and Kavanagh to Yeats. And the Yanks and Brits can, for the most part, understand what the Irish poet is talking about, without the time consuming and always complicating intervention of a translator.

In recent history Korean poets have had no such luck. Korea, whose isolationist policies had led the country to be nicknamed 'the Hermit Kingdom', was annexed by Japan in 1910—the British had also been eyeing it up for colonisation—and remained so until Japan's collapse in 1945. Then the country was immediately divided and became a pawn in the incipient Cold War; the Soviets accepted the Japanese surrender in the North while the Americans accepted it in the South. Korea was immediately partitioned along the famous 38th parallel. And it wasn't long before the next war.

For most people the word 'Korea' conjures up the TV series M⋆A⋆S⋆H, grainy footage of refugees filing along country roads and the ridiculous haircut sported by North Korea's Dear Leader, Kim Yong-il, the world's last Stalinist. But, in the West, Korean culture remains obscure to all but the expert few. Its literary culture in particular is hugely rich; *The Jiki*, a collection of excerpts from the most revered Buddhist monks—an important influence on Japan's Zen Buddhism—was the first book ever printed using moveable metal type in 1377. What Guttenburg would discover decades later, the Koreans did first. In this context this journal's birth is to be celebrated. The fact that it is so beautifully produced, as one would perhaps expect from a journal emanating from Harvard University, and is of such quality in terms of the material published in its inaugural issue, also bode well. *Azalea* is a quite overwhelming collection of poems, fiction, photographs, memoir, book reviews and essays. 'Yi Jong-yi's Family', one of five poems by Ko Un (born 1933) translated here by Brother Anthony of Taizé and Lee Sang-Wha, brings us face to face with all that's worst about war.

They walked all the way from Chinnamp'o in North Korea
to Hongsong in South Korea's Ch'ungchong Province.
They walked and walked,
for twenty days they fled.

Yi Jon-hae
and her sister Yi Jong-yi
with their parents following them.

All day long walking with nothing to eat.
When they found a well
they drank then walked on in the flesh-biting cold.

They dreaded the American troops
so they smeared their clothes
with their own shit.

They spread soot from kitchen chimneys
over their faces.
The mother became

a beggar-mom,
her daughters beggar kids.

Their bodies stank of shit.
Instead of American troops, the dogs came running...

No doubt much of the poem's original linguistic zip and crackle is lost in the move from the Korean to English. But something else is born, and those grainy shadow people who for me, until now, only existed in old photographs and footage are given a voice. Intellectually the Korean War was (and remains) a hugely problematic question for liberal leftists; the image of Korean peasant children smearing themselves in their own faeces out of fear of attack by US soldiers is a horrific one. And yet from this juncture it is clear to all but the most ossified apologists for Stalinism that it would have been a much better outcome for the workers and peasants of the Democratic People's Republic of (North) Korea if the American led force had been completely victorious and the 'socialist paradise', in which they're still imprisoned, had ceased to exist half a century ago.

Another very different poem which I thoroughly enjoyed was Hwang In-sook's 'I Wish To Be Born As A Cat': "I might wander the empty fields / in cold rain and gusting wind, / but not a single bit of my fur will get wet, / I'll dream / the dream of running in a sunlit field / after the magpie I missed that day." Poets tend to identify with cats; perhaps because, like cats, most poets survive on the scraps society throws them. Dogs are team players, but cats are ruthless individualists. And there is something about that which appeals to poets.

There is, of course, a large and increasingly influential Korean population in the United States itself. So it's no surprise that some Korean poets, such as Chonggi Mah (born 1939) should turn their attention to what John McCain and Barack Obama like to call Main Street:

from THE FALL OF PATERSON

*"The great city split into three parts and the cities of the
nations collapsed." (Rev. 16:19)*

1

The streets of Paterson, New Jersey
are so dangerous you cannot walk alone even by day.
Flowers and squirrels, pigeons and clouds,
parks and benches and lawns are all rotting
and what poets called "beautiful things" have left.

The city's little waterfall used to sing a high-pitched chorus,
the sky above the waterfall where a doctor strolled in the 1940s,
within that sky the water daily becoming a rainbow, but
now even the fresh foam is a dumping ground of dry ruins.
City of poverty, crime, drugs, and AIDS,
only hatred, insomnia, and the gunshots of fear remain…

Despite or perhaps because of its nowheresville status Paterson has
come to occupy quite an important place in recent American
culture: it is the racism-ridden town described in the Bob Dylan
song 'Hurricane' and I'm guessing that the doctor in the second
stanza, second line is William Carlos Williams, the great American
Modernist and author of the epic titled, you guessed it, *Paterson*.
For me, the most powerful line in Mah's poem is the exquisite
"what poets called "beautiful things" have left". Chonggi Mah
worked as a doctor himself, so he obviously feels a particular
affinity with Williams. The most striking thing about Mah's poetry,
though, is the interplay between his profoundly Korean sensibility
and urban America at its roughest.

Other highlights include a very interesting essay by Robert
Pinsky, 'Peace, Poetry and Negation', in which he investigates
everything from Buddhism to Wallace Stevens to Thomas Jefferson
to W.B Yeats to Robert Lowell to Czeslaw Milosz. This journal is
a treasure, and given the culture it's dedicated to, has much work
to do in its task of bringing Korean literature out into the light.

Vallum magazine (Montreal, Winter 2008-2009)

From Tyburn To A Tin Box

Cromwell's Head by JONATHAN FITZGIBBONS

Oliver Cromwell is—it almost goes without saying—a hugely divisive figure. In Ireland his opinion poll ratings remain even lower than those of soon-to-be-former President George W. Bush and only slightly higher than those of that famous Austrian advocate of a very different type of European unity: the late Adolf Hitler. Indeed, the massacres that followed Cromwell's storming of Drogheda on the coincidental date of September 11th 1649, and the generalised butchery of civilians which also took place at Wexford a month later, has led us to see Cromwell as something of a Hitler figure. The mere mention of his name can still start fights in pubs, something even post-budget Brian Cowen can only aspire to. Fitzgibbons tells the story of Cromwell, and how his legacy continues to be argued about all these centuries later, by following the journey of the Lord Protector's head, from its detachment from the rest of his body at Tyburn "on the cold winter's morning of Wednesday 30 January 1661" to its final burial in a tin box at his alma mater, Sidney Sussex College in 1960. Its burial there was arranged by Canon Horace Wilkinson. Cromwell's head had been in his family since his grandfather, Josiah, purchased it in 1815: "Lovingly preserved in a small oak box, the head would be produced as a conversation piece at private gatherings of friends and family"! Those who separate others from their heads—as Cromwell did with King Charles I—often end up headless themselves. Fitzgibbon's description of Cromwell's decapitation is as chilling as that January morning must have been: "this would be no ordinary execution since all three of the condemned had been deceased for quite some time. Cromwell had now been dead for over two years; his son-in-law Henry Ireton had succumbed to a fever while on campaign in Ireland in November 1651; John Bradshaw, famous for his role as Lord President of the High Court of Justice that tried Charles I, passed away fifteen months earlier...A Spanish merchant named Samuel Sainthill gives a lurid eyewitness account: The odious carcasses... were hanged by the neck, from morning till four in the afternoon. Cromwell in a green-seare cloth, very fresh, embalmed; Ireton having been buried long, hung like a dried rat... Bradshaw, in his winding sheet...his nose perished, having wet the sheet through."

Cromwell's posthumous decapitation was part of the Restoration era backlash against everything he represented. It's important to remember that in the England of his day, Cromwell was a figure of the left rather than the right. He tore down the old order of the 'divine right of kings' and could be seen as the man who invented parliamentary democracy. He is to this day hated by monarchists and many Tories for precisely this reason. So, the worst atrocities in Irish history were committed by a man who was, as the Marxists would say, a progressive rather than a reactionary. Cromwell's legacy is complicated and then some. Jonathan Fitzgibbons brings all that complexity nicely to life here.

Galway Advertiser, December 2008

Tammy Wynette meets
the Real IRA

American Skin by KEN BRUEN

Right now, in that corner of a Galwegian field that is forever Tigh Neachtains, someone is no doubt busy talking up his or her novel-in-progress. It is, very likely, such a complex interplay of influences: Kafka meets Virginia Woolf meets Herman Melville outside St. Nicholas's Church on a Wednesday, that the only way its author can properly protect the book's artistic integrity is by leaving it forever unwritten. Some novels are so perfect, ink can never be allowed to make its way onto paper. Ken Bruen is many miles removed from the frustrated literary elitist parodied above. Hugely prolific, he has published dozens of novels and shows no sign of slowing down. Bruen is most appreciated for his detective fiction. His Jack Taylor series, which follows the adventures of a wayward former member of An Garda Siochaina, has been particularly popular. But Bruen is also sometimes a social realist, passing cutting comment on Galway as it has become; sometimes a kind of barroom surrealist, taking the reader into those corners of the psyche where strange and terrible things happen all the time. *American Skin* is very much in this surreal vein and has been compared to William Burrough's 1959 heroin driven classic, *Naked Lunch*, which must surely rank as one of the strangest books ever written. It is no surprise that, in Bruen's hands, the America dreams of his characters very quickly become nightmares populated by all that's worst. The writer most influencing Ken Bruen these days seems to be Pat McCabe. However, a crime is the engine driving *American Skin*'s plot. Steve-O Blake from Galway is on the run after a bank heist, hoping to disappear in the Arizona desert and re-emerge as a fully fledged American. Unfortunately for Steve-O the only thing that runs smoothly in Ken Bruen's books is the road to hell. The plot jerks here and there and the pages are peppered with music references, everyone from Emmylou Harris to Teenage Fanclub. You never know what's coming next, and that's as it should be. Bruen introduces us to John A. Stapleton, a dissident republican bank robber for whom "The Peace Talks were like the worst news". He's bad enough. But at least he's a variety of politically obsessed sociopath that we're familiar enough with in Ireland. Far more disturbing is Dade, who bears "more than a passing resemblance to Christopher Walken"—never a good sign!—and is obsessed with the music of Tammy Wynette. During a stint in jail "a black guy knocked out his [Dade's] teeth". Dade is "a leading light in a white supremacist gang" and his response is savage. He takes "the guy's eyes out with a spoon". In a Ken Bruen novel one never expects everything to turn out okay. He isn't one to tie up a story by having Dick Van Dyke turn up on the last page singing 'Put On A Happy Face!' But in *American Skin* he *really* takes us into the dark. A must for all fans.

Galway Advertiser, October 2008

Poetry to save lives

The Boy in the Ring by DAVE LORDAN

In the small world that is the Irish poetry scene Dave Lordan is, to say the least of it, an unusual case. His poetic imagination is politically engaged in a way that sets him apart from the vast majority of his contemporaries. Lordan was born in Clonakilty in 1975 and now lives in Dublin. For Irish poets of the previous couple of generations, opposition to the political and cultural status quo (whatever form that opposition might take) was more or less a given. Until the 1990s there was, for most, no way to be a poet in Ireland and not be opposed to things as they were.

The Irish feminist movement of the 1970s and '80s had its poetic counterpart in Eavan Boland's 1982 collection *Night Feed*, the Catholic church was pretty wickedly satirised in poems such as Paul Durcan's 'Priest Accused of Not Wearing Condom', and the brave new Ireland of the late 1970s was starkly taken to task in poems such as 'Cuchulainn' by Michael O'Loughlin: "At eleven-fifteen on a Tuesday morning / with the wind blowing fragments of concrete / Into eyes already battered and bruised / By four tightening walls / In a flat in a tower-block / Named after an Irish Patriot / Who died with your name on his lips…"

Suffering poverty is one thing: poets have a long history of being fairly okay with poverty, both their own and other people's. But living under the then very real yoke of the Catholic Church—the constitutional ban on divorce, homosexual acts between consenting men illegal until 1993, the sale of condoms completely illegal until 1979—was bound to provoke opposition from artists. I think it was Trotsky who wrote that artists are petit-bourgeois in revolt against the role society is trying to force them into, or words to that effect. Until at least the late 1970s all Irish writers had to

87

worry about censorship, and Irish women writers had to constantly fight against the silence which had been imposed on their mothers and grandmothers. In the Ireland of the recent past if you were a poet, or artist of any sort, what you were *for* may not have been at all clear, but you typically knew what you were against.

In the past twenty years many of these issues have either ceased to be or been greatly ameliorated. The church is nothing like the force it was. Censorship is a distant abstraction to young writers starting out now. These days a poet is far more likely to draw the wrath of the left, for not toeing some 'party line', than he or she is to be condemned by the powers that be, who are, to be frank, so secure in their position of ideological supremacy that they don't care what poets say about them. Yes, free market capitalism has, with impunity, put its hands into pretty much every area of Irish life over the past decade or so. Most artistic types don't like this, or at least think it has gone too far. But they are not alone in not having a clue what is to be done about it.

Voting for Enda Kenny (with a bit of Éamon Gilmore thrown in) seems unlikely to change much. And to the bulk of artists, as to most people, the existing far left seems to be more about the past than the future. Even the most apolitical poet knows about what Stalin did to artists, and no one wants to revisit that. Those few who do loudly engage with political issues tend to follow the formula of writing a stream of vituperative letters to the editor (everywhere from the *Irish Times* to the *Longford Independent*) in which they often conclude by sniping at their fellow scribes for not being similarly *engagé*. For most, excepting those tragic few on the far left who are impressed, it is clear that this sort of 'political engagement' is more about death than life. 'Notice me!' the sad scribe shrieks. 'Before they screw down my coffin lid!' But the world has more important things to attend to. And so the scribe shrieks all the louder. The value of the politically engaged writer has rarely been more open to question than in Ireland right now. In this context Dave Lordan's explosion onto the Irish poetry scene over the past couple of years has been a revelation. Towards the end of 2005 he won the Patrick Kavanagh Award. This March he won the Strong Award for Best First Collection, and was also shortlisted for the *Irish Times* Poetry Now Award, which was won last year by a little known Co. Derry poet by the name of Séamus Heaney. Lordan's rise is also proof that what is sometimes called the literary establishment is very open indeed to good political poems, however revolutionary they may be. It would perhaps have been more politically advantageous for his comrades if, when his first book appeared, instead of Lordan being brought to Dún Laoghaire to be given a big award, all copies of *The Boy in the Ring* had been seized in an early morning Special Branch raid on Salmon Poetry's headquarters in Clare and Lordan himself exiled to Inisboffin. But it was not to be.

In his poetry Lordan is open about his politics. His point of view is usually that of participant rather than bystander, as in the case of 'Migrant's March, Genoa, July 19, 2001':

> The slogans surging up the back of fifty thousand throats
> to greet them in our provisional republic.
>
> *Free-Free Kurdistan.*
> *So-So-Solidarité.*
> *A- Anti- Anti-capitalista.*
> *Un altro mondo é possible.*
> *Noi siamo tutti clandestini.*
>
> A language we all understand.
> Is there any such thing as Ireland?

The closing couplet well brings to life the way participation in big political movements can help us transcend the apparently commonsense realities around us. The experimental five-page '*Excerpt from* Reflections on Shannon' and 'The hunger striker sings his death' also both overtly engage with politics in a way that your typical poet believer in all things *Irish Times* would not:

> I ask you again
> What the fuck is silence;
> And who ever heard
> The dead requesting it?

I have, on occasion, heard Lordan's poems criticised for being somewhat bombastic and more than a little relentless. It's important to know that Lordan considers the 'stage'—i.e. reading his poems aloud to an audience—to be more important than the page—i.e. having his poems quietly read from a book by solitary passive readers. When he is on form, he is one of the best performers Irish poetry has to offer. I once saw him perform 'The hunger striker sings his death' to a Galway audience which included a woman from a Protestant unionist background in the North who up to that point had more or less believed that the H-Block hunger strikers were just a bunch of guys who had starved themselves to death years ago to make some obscure political point. After the reading this same woman turned to me and said: "Now I get it." As a poet Lordan has an ability to animate a subject in a way that far outstrips most of even the better public speakers on the left.

He gives his reader/listener the feeling that the people he writes about are not simply pawns in the political argument which undeniably *does* underpin many of his poems: he also cares about them as human beings. Lordan is an engaged witness to what is going on, rather than a propagandist trying to fit the world into some pre-conceived scheme. It is true that some of his poems are better heard aloud than read on the page but, as I've said, that is part of his plan. Lordan is one of a group of younger poets emerging in Ireland right now for whom reading their poems to live audiences is at least as important as being read on the page in the quiet of the reader's living room. Others would include Cork poet Billy Ramsell who was shortlisted for the same Strong Award which Lordan won. One blogger commented that this year's Strong Award seemed to represent the arrival in Ireland of "some sort of performance poetry". And they were, in a sense, on the button. Many of the old boundaries have been eroded or kicked away, and the Irish poetry world is undeniably a more open, less snobbish place than at any other time in its history.

There have, yes, been one or two old guarders keen to pour ignorant scorn on the open mic and poetry slam scene which has sprung up in most of the key urban centres in Ireland over the past five years: they are the sort of people who would no doubt amend Yeats's exhortation to future generations from "Irish poets, learn your trade" to 'Younger poets, know your place'. A professor of Irish Studies based at a major American university—a pillar of the literary establishment, if you will—recently likened the aforementioned naysayers to those old men who like to whinge away to themselves about how 'There's never anything any good on the telly these days!' Sadly, they have had some (albeit ineffectual) encouragement from those who should know better.

In 2006 a poet member of a many-initialled Trotskyist group published an article in which it was argued that young poets would be better off going along to hear an elderly socialist playwright read his work in a small provincial hotel than wasting their time constantly reading their own work to audiences. Controversy ensued in the pages of *The Irish Times, Poetry Ireland News* and elsewhere. It is true that young poets should read the great poetry of the past: absolutely. But when a member of a Trotskyist group starts running around trying to stir up deference among the young, we have, to paraphrase Evelyn Waugh, ended up in a very queer street indeed. But I suppose we all make mistakes. In contrast, Dave Lordan has been a staunch advocate of the new poetic openness, even when this has meant not exactly toeing the party line.

And his best poems seal the argument. His 'Explanations of War' is one of the finest anti-war poems I have read in years:

See all those bright lights whizzing around in the sky—
They are only the stars throwing a party.
And the shaking you feel beneath you,
The shaking that jars your teeth and your bones—
That is only the way the earth dances.
And the bangs and roars, the cracks and blasts and booms—
These are only the sounds of little spirits tuning their instruments...

But by far Lordan's greatest quality as a poet is his empathy. George Orwell once wrote that he found it hard to imagine that the typical "polysyllable-chewing Marxist" of the 1930s could possibly have been motivated by a love of anything, let alone the working class. He came to the conclusion that capitalism offended many of them not because it was unjust but because it was untidy. Lordan is a different sort of Marxist, and one rarely spotted in the English language poetry world. He has a genuine anarchic love of those who, as your Auntie Mary might put it, 'give us all a bad name'. His 'Ode on de winning of de Entente Florale' ironically and viciously celebrates Clonakilty's win in that competition by giving voice to the, at times, Waffen SS-like prejudices of the organising committee: "Told ye so. Told ye we could win it / 'Spite de filth o' de likes o' ye / With yere baseball caps and yere baggy pants, / Yere ghetto blasters and yere nigger music.../ And de trainee hoors hangin' offa ye." Lordan's use of the demotic brings to mind the work of poets such as Linton Kwesi Johnson and Tony Harrison.

And indeed, if English as it is spoken by the Afro-Caribbean community in London and the white working class in West Yorkshire can be brought into poetry, then why not Clonakilty? I trust the committee who masterminded the town's Entente Florale triumph are suitably proud of Lordan.

His empathy is at its sharpest when dealing with the issue of suicide, which a number of the poems here do. Far ahead of unaffordable house prices and traffic jams, youth suicide has been the real curse of Ireland's Tiger years. 'Mail for a dead guide' is written in the form of a letter to a friend who killed himself. Lordan is the first Irish poet to seriously and credibly engage with this subject. He is breaking new poetic ground in the way that, say, Cathal Ó Searcaigh was when he began publishing poems about being a young gay man growing up in rural Ireland back in the late 1970s. Lordan's empathy is born of the fact that he is never an outsider to the issues he writes about, and has clearly done near deadly battle with his own demons in the past.

> I finally get to this morning
> but cringe at thoughts of my father
> at the front door explaining
> my mother's Antigonian wailing…
>
> In true Irish martyr fashion
> I've decided not to give a warning.
> ['Dying for Ireland']

Lordan has until recently been best known as a fairly brash political poet. But there is a huge vulnerability there too, which will, I think, be the making of him as a poet. It has enabled him to take his poetry into the until now uncharted terrain of modern Irish loneliness and despair at their worst. Every secondary school in Ireland should, as a matter of urgency, book Dave Lordan for a visit under the Writers in Schools scheme. We all know the old Auden cliché about poetry making nothing happen, but in this case it might actually save lives.

Red Banner magazine, September 2008

Galway launch of poems from Guantánamo Bay

Poems from Guantánamo—The Detainees Speak edited by Mark Falkoff has its Galway launch, organised by Amnesty International in association with Over The Edge, in the Galway Amnesty Café and Shop, Middle Street on Thursday June 26th at 7pm. Local poets Rita Ann Higgins, Mary O'Malley, Elaine Feeney, Gary King & Stephen Murray will each read a poem from the anthology, as will visiting American poet Charlene Spearen and Sheik Khaled, Imam of Galway Mosque. The MC for the evening will be my good self. All are welcome.

The abuses, such as waterboarding, which have taken place at the Guantánamo facility have been a disaster for the United States. On the morning of Wednesday September 12th 2001, the US Government undeniably held the high ground morally. All but the most knee-jerk America haters where horrified by the coldblooded slaughter by Al Queda of almost three thousand American office workers. But that moral advantage has been totally squandered by the Bush administration. During these past few years we have had the spectacle of western liberals and leftists lining up to attend anti-war meetings addressed by speakers from Hezbollah and the likes of George Galloway MP, who once boasted about the night he spent on "the crowded dance floor" of a North African nightclub with Tariq Aziz, one of Sadaam Hussein's leading hatchet men. The mere fact of them being opposed to the Bush administration and the Iraq war has allowed some of the worst people in the world, whose opposition to war and torture is selective indeed, to gain an entirely undeserved credibility. International politics has become a stark choice between the ghastly and the even worse. It's a very good thing indeed that both Barack Obama and John McCain have promised to close the Guantánamo Bay facility. If these past seven years have taught us anything, it is that you do not defeat anti-democratic fruitcakes like Al Queda by adopting anti-democratic methods yourself. In a democratic society, which the United States so loudly proclaims itself to be, the right to a fair trial, denied to the Guantánamo detainees, must be absolute, available to everyone however difficult the circumstances. And torture is always out.

Poems from Guantánamo contains poems by seventeen detainees with accompanying biographical notes. It bears witness to the suffering that goes on there daily. The poems vary greatly in style. Martin Mubanga's 'Terrorist 2003' is what we would call a slam or performance poem: "America sucks, America chills, / While d' blood of d' Muslims is forever getting spilled, / In d' streets of Nablus, in d' streets of Jenin, / Yeahhhhhhh! You know what I mean." Shaikh Adburraheem Muslim Dost's 'Cup Poem 1' is a much quieter almost haiku: "What kind of spring is this, / Where there are no flowers and / The air is filled with a miserable smell?" This beautifully produced book makes the reader realise that those detained at Guantánamo Bay are not mere statistics, pawns in a war or political argument, but human beings with the same everyday hopes and fears as the rest of us.

Galway Advertiser, June 2008

The Lost World of
Francis Ledwidge

The Ledwidge Treasury—Selected Poems

Francis Ledwidge was born in Meath, and died at Ypres in 1917. He was three weeks shy of thirty when a shell killed him and several other members of his regiment. He had published one slight collection, *Songs of The Fields*. A second, *Songs of Peace*, was at the printers. He was an unlikely poet. His father, an agricultural labourer, died when he was four, leaving the family destitute. Ledwidge wrote his first poem, 'A Little Boy In The Morning', as an act of 'rebellion' when he was sixteen and employed as a grocer's apprentice. He sympathised with the locked out workers in 1913 and was a member of the Irish Volunteers. He initially opposed John Redmond's support for Britain in the Great War, but entertained the notion that Britain might ask the Irish Volunteers and the Ulster Volunteers to defend the Irish coast. In this way, he hoped, sectarian division would be overcome. Despite his reservations, Ledwidge enlisted. But the contradictions continued: his most famous poem is 'Thomas McDonagh', inspired by his friend and fellow poet's execution after the 1916 Rising: "He shall not hear the bittern cry / In the wild sky, where he is lain". McDonagh was shot by members of the army of which Ledwidge was a serving member.

The Ledwidge Treasury incorporates poems from 'Songs of The Fields' and 'Songs of Peace', alongside eleven poems—'Last Songs'—which Ledwidge wrote towards the very end. They are sandwiched between an introduction by Seamus Heaney and a moving afterword by Dermot Bolger. Heaney is honest about Ledwidge's limitations, describing him as: "neither a very strong nor a very original talent." In its weaker moments his poetry is sentimental and relies on rhymes that now sound amateurish: "wing" and "spring"; "song" and "long". But Heaney goes on to champion Ledwidge's "tendermindedness towards the predicament of others" and "ethically unsparing attitude towards the self". He observes that the "meaning of [Ledwidge's] choice has lost resonance because the concept of personal integrity as a relevant factor in political decision has been gradually eroding: a Marxist-influenced consensus tends to put the onus on the individual to make a correct theoretical assessment of what is historically progressive". Heaney is right. These days the whole truth is often more obstacle than ally for the Left-leaning poet: the genocide in Darfur is 'inconvenient' because it is perpetuated by Moslems on other Moslems and can't be easily blamed on George W. Bush. Mention Darfur and the Left-leaning poet will typically change the subject to the more politically convenient Palestine or Iraq. On its own the beautiful and powerful 'Thomas McDonagh' is proof Ledwidge was a more moral poet than that. And the exquisite 'The Wife of Lew'—"for her voice they made a linnet sing"—is as good a love poem as you'll find.

Ledwidge never reached poetic maturity. If he had come back from the war, he would've come back changed, as a poet and as a man. But the Modern poet he might have been was lost that day in 1917, when the twentieth century was still just young enough to allow him to be the humane poet he was.

Galway Advertiser, September 2007

The Racket Made
By Paul Muldoon

The New Yorker magazine observed recently that Racket are probably the only garage-rock band in the world with a Pulitzer Prize Winning Poet as a member. Paul Muldoon penned the lyrics for Racket's first two albums, *Resistance* (2006) and the recently released follow up *Standing Room Only*. When he's not trying to get the hang of his reissue 1952 Butterscotch Telecaster guitar, Muldoon is busy being by far the most the obvious challenger to Seamus Heaney for the mantle of the leading Irish poet. Since his first collection, *The New Weather*, arrived courtesy of Faber and Faber in 1973, Muldoon has published nine subsequent poetry collections, including *Moy Sand and Gravel*, which won him the 2003 Pulitzer Prize. Born in 1951 in County Armagh, Muldoon has lived in the United States since 1987, where he is a Professor at Princeton University. He has also been Professor of Poetry at Oxford, a position previously held by the likes of Robert Graves, W.H. Auden and Mathew Arnold, none of whom (as far as anyone knows) ever wrote lyrics for a garage-rock band.

At first glance Muldoon is a somewhat unlikely lyricist. Reviewing *Moy Sand and Gravel,* the *New York Times* said "Muldoon writes poems that ask for a highly qualified reader. If you knew everything Muldoon has ever known…had met everyone Muldoon has ever met and could make every mental connection Muldoon has ever clicked on, you'd be in the running to qualify". This is taking it a bit far. It would be wrong to call Muldoon's poems obscure; they are mostly pretty accessible. But his wordplay and linguistically subversive use of puns and clichés— "You can lead a horse to water but you can't make it hold / its nose to the grindstone"—puts him in a different camp altogether to a crowd-pleasing, satirical poet such as Paul Durcan, whose poems one could easily imagine doubling as lyrics for strange contemporary folk-songs. So what of the music Racket make? Muldoon himself describes their sound as "Cole Porter meets prog and punk, or Ira Gershwin glam and grunge."

With Stephen Allen on keyboards, Bobby Lewis on drums, Lee Mathew on vocals and guitar, Nigel Smith on bass and Paul Muldoon on guitar, there is a definite post-punk feel to many of Racket's songs. But their influences are varied, marrying as they do the apparent opposites of prog-rock and punk. In 'Meat and Drink' they sound like a cross between The Jesus And Mary Chain and The Smiths with Brian Ferry thrown in as lead singer for good measure. 'The Wrong Man' is the song The Red Hot Chilli Peppers might have written if they'd been from Essex rather than L.A. Muldoon's lyrics are always sharp and witty: "You showed up in that silk shirt / It looked a dead cert / We're in the home straight / We're near the winning post // At the Ascot Gold Cup / I was an also ran / Someone's set me up / You've got the wrong man." It is a brave step indeed for a fifty six year old Princeton Poetry Professor to go on tour with his garage-rock band. Paul Muldoon's latest venture is further confirmation that the best poets are usually those who've learnt not to take themselves too seriously.

Galway Advertiser, August 2007

Taking Arms Against
A Sea of Troubles

Neoconservatism: Why We Need It by DOUGLAS MURRAY

It would be understatement of the decade to say that the likes of Paul Wolfowitz and Richard Perle, who in the aftermath of the Al-Qaeda mass murder on September 11th 2001 decisively influenced US foreign policy, have lately been subject to a certain amount of criticism. For the past five years the neoconservatives have served as pet hate-figures for the placard-waving 'anti-war' Left. Judge a man by his friends, but while you're at it, take a good look at his enemies. Of the neocons foes former US Attorney General, Ramsay Clark, is perhaps the most indicative. On page seventy six Douglas Murray points out that, during the Clinton years, when they were away from the centre of power:

"In petitions, letters to the newspapers, speeches and articles, Wolfowitz, Perle, and Jeane Kirkpatrick were among neoconservatives who consistently lobbied for armed intervention to halt the progress of ethnic cleansing and slaughter. 'After seven years of aggression and genocide in the Balkans, the removal of Milosevic provides the only genuine possibility of a durable peace', they wrote in a 1998 letter to President Clinton."

Ramsay Clark took the diametrically opposed view. After attending Slobadon Milosevic's funeral in Belgrade on March 18th 2006, Clark told *Associated Press* that:

"It is critically important to remember his struggle to preserve Yugoslavia. He [Milosevic] became president at a time of greatest crisis. Everyone knew his health was failing but he was not granted proper medical care. Amid the struggle, his heart gave up."

That Milosevic's "struggle to preserve Yugoslavia" involved a bit of genocide here and there is, it seems, of no consequence to Lyndon Johnson's distinguished former Attorney General. Of course Ramsay Clark is not exactly representative of the broad 'anti-war' movement. His association with the pro-North Korea *Workers World Party* marks him out as one of the most exotic flowers to have sprung up in the desert that is the post-cold war Left. But the broad 'anti-war' Left have presented Clark to the world as if he were someone to be taken seriously. In January 2003, two months before the invasion of Iraq, 'peace-activist' Mary Kelly attacked a US Air Force plane with an axe at Shannon Airport on the West coast of Ireland. I have no problem with acts of civil disobedience as part of a political campaign; even in the most open democracy things rarely change by voting alone. My initial sympathies were more with Mary Kelly than against her. Then, in the court case which ensued, she produced her star witness: Ramsay Clark, who took the stand to tell us: "If you ever want peace on earth, you don't prosecute the people taking action to protect peace." No mention was made of Clark's enthusiasm for Slobadon Milosevic; not one word in the liberal columns of the *Irish Times* or the Trotskyist *Socialist Worker*. Nor was it pointed out that one cannot credibly describe oneself as 'anti-war' if one thinks what Milosevic did to Bosnia was a job well done, as Clark apparently does. Instead Deirdre Clancy of Indymedia Ireland gushed about how: "The sage-like Ramsey Clark (former U.S. Attorney General and longtime peace campaigner) testified for 30 minutes about the adverse effects of U.S. foreign policy".

This made me reconsider my own absolute in-all-circumstances opposition to US military intervention. I too had opposed the NATO bombing of Serbia in 1999, which led to Milosevic's forced withdrawal from Kosovo and eventual overthrow. The argument had been that the NATO action would only strengthen Milosevic and lead to more not less suffering for the Kosovo Albanians. I was clearly wrong. On this one at least Richard Perle, Paul Wolfowitz and Jeane Kirkpatrick were correct. There's a sentence I never thought I'd write.

The Left's fawning attitude toward Ramsay Clark raises profound questions, which go beyond the specifics of the situation in Kosovo.

I had known about the deadly Stalinist combination of lies and mass murder ever since I was a raw fifteen year old recruit to Trotskyism back in 1982. I knew my *Animal Farm* and my *Nineteen Eighty-Four*. But with the collapse of the Soviet Union, I'd thought Left wing lies and Left wing apologia for mass murder were something from terrible times past. I now began to ask myself whether there is something inherent in Left wing thinking which, where it holds sway, makes lies and mass murder likely if not inevitable.

If one wrote a letter to the *Irish Times* pointing out Ramsay Clark's support for the genocidal racist Milosevic, one would at best be accused in devastated whispers by sandal-clad ladies of 'giving comfort to the other [pro-war] side'; at worst one would be loudly denounced for having become a pro-imperialist lackey. This is the way the far Left typically reacts to inconvenient truths. This rabid intolerance goes a long way to explaining how Stalin, Mao, Enver Hoxha, and Pol Pot came to happen; and how Robert Mugabe continues to happen. For all his monumental faults, George W. Bush is without doubt preferable to a government of all the Mary Kellys, all the Ramsay Clarks—more words I never thought I'd write; the erosion of civil liberties which has occurred in the US since 9/11 is nothing compared to what the far Left would do were it ever again to stumble into power. All anyone who doubts this need do is wander along to the next far left 'anti-war' meeting to take place in your town and ask the top table the question:"what would you have done to save the Kosovo Albanians?" When they fob you off, ask it again and again. Then look around the room at the dumb, unblinking eyes of the rank and file and ask yourself what life would be like if these people had at their disposal all the resources of the FBI and the CIA?

Last December, on foot of a review I first published in *Books In Canada* of Anna Funder's *Stasiland*, I received an e-mail from the chairperson of the local anti-war campaign here. He said that he had heard I had "joyfully attack[ed] the GDR in some article." He wasn't happy. I was aware that this individual had for many years been a member of the Communist Party, but I was surprised nevertheless. If he had state power, I would no doubt have felt the full force of his unhappiness in decidedly less abstract terms. Two weeks ago the same person published a letter in the local paper protesting against the annual air show which takes place here in June. He objected to the fact that US military aircraft were taking part. He said that, given what is going on in Iraq, this is a "moral issue".

I'm sorry, but the guy who supported torture and tyranny in Poland, Bulgaria, East Germany, Hungary, and the Soviet Union is in no position to give the average Joe and Josephine, who turn out to see the air show each year in their tens of thousands, a lecture about morality. And given that his opposition to torture is entirely conditional on who's doing the torturing; if it were being done by his Stasi or KGB pals he'd be absolutely fine with it; he is perhaps not best placed to lecture the US Government about extraordinary rendition either. But, again, if one were to write to the local paper raising these issues, one would be accused of, among other things, McCarthyism. The Left is more often than not the enemy of truth, the bully's friend. That has been my experience. So in making his case for neoconservatism, Douglas Murray was in every sense pushing an open door, where I was concerned. Does he convince me? Well, if I'm honest, no more than I had already convinced myself.

In the first chapter, Murray looks at the roots of American neoconservatism, going back to the late 1940s. Irving Kristol is accurately described as "godfather of neoconservatism". Kristol's background is crucial. He was not from the traditionalist Republican right, but began his political life as a Trotskyist at City College New York in the late 1930s. A fellow student at CCNY was Saul Bellow, who was also briefly a Trotskyist, but whose own political ideas later similarly lurched to the right. Max Eastman once said only those who have had close involvement with the communist movement can know just how manipulative, how sinister it can be. The average politician, liberal or conservative, will tell you many little lies. But you will get over it. You may even vote them in again and live to tell the tale. However the lies the far Left tells are spiritually destructive, because they typically start out talking about a world of perfect human equality, before going on to say that to achieve this perfect world we must for now give 'critical support' to this or that horrible tyrant. Murray delineates how: "From the beginnings of his career as a writer and journalist in the late 1940s, Kristol had become a forceful and lucid anti-communist." Despite this Kristol was queasy about Joseph McCarthy:

"the truth is that the problem existed, was growing, had nuclear weaponry, and possessed a great many supporters in the heart of America. For those like Kristol, living through the period and seeking to retain traditional liberal Americanism while utterly opposing communism, Senator McCarthy was still an unappealing figure, described by Kristol in one essay as a "vulgar demagogue."

However, in the same essay Kristol went on to say:

"there is one thing that the American people know about Senator McCarthy: he, like them, is unequivocally anti-Communist. About the spokesmen for American Liberalism, they feel they know no such thing. And with some justification."

A similar relativism affects the contemporary Left. These days it is usually the liberal or socialist you'll hear waffling about how the recent Knighthood for Salman Rushdie is grossly insensitive to the feelings of Moslem people. The fact that there is nothing liberal about defending those who would interfere with Rushdie's right to write whatever comes into his imagination is a fact which will get you no hearing from much of the post-9/11 Left, as they try to cuddle up to the Mullahs.

Murray shows how, as the cold war went on, the position of Irving Kristol and his co-thinkers hardened: "By its consistent refusal to adequately condemn Nazism's single moral equivalent in Russia, liberalism had shown that it possessed none of the attributes its name suggested. By undermining the society that was defending true liberal values from the threat of communist tyranny, it had shown its flaws and deceits." Most on the Trotskyist Left continued to argue a position of 'critical support' for the Soviet Union against the United States right up to the end of the cold war. At bottom this meant that, while they agreed that socialism in the Soviet Union was monstrously deformed, it was still preferable to a capitalist society such as that in the USA. To believe this is to believe that living in Communist Poland during the Cold War would have been preferable to living in, for example, capitalist Belgium during the same time period. It was quite simply an insane world view. However, not all Trotskyists held this position. On May 9th 1951 one member of the Fourth International resigned in protest at the organisation's continued 'critical support for the Soviet Union.' Her resignation letter, sent to the leadership of the group's American section, the Socialist Workers Party, had this to say:

"As far back as 1927, Trotsky, in reply to a disloyal question put to him in the Political Bureau by Stalin, stated his views as follows: For the socialist fatherland, yes! For the Stalinist regime, no! Now, twenty three years later Stalin has left nothing of the socialist fatherland. It has been replaced by the enslavement and degradation of the people by the Stalinist autocracy. This is the state you propose to defend in the war, which you are already defending in Korea."

The woman who wrote this was Trotsky's widow, Natalia. I doubt Natalia Trotsky would have any time at all for Mary Kelly's pal "The sage-like Ramsey Clark". She had more spine in her than that. Her argument echoes the earlier thesis of Max Shachtman, who argued in 1940 that, after the Hitler-Stalin pact, the Soviet Union was no longer in any sense defensible. Shachtman is a hugely important figure, the real link-man between Trotskyism and neoconservatism. Jean Kirkpatrick, Paul Wolfowitz and Richard Perle were all members of "Social Democrats USA" in the early Seventies, the group then led by Max Shachtman. They initially supported the 1972 and 1976 Presidential campaigns of anti-communist Democrat Senator, Henry 'Scoop' Jackson, before switching to Ronald Reagan in 1980. They played a key role in giving the Reagan administration the mettle to end what they saw as the appeasing policies of Nixon and Carter. There would be no more détente. By 1991 the Soviet Union was gone. Natalia Trotsky died in Paris in 1962. Had she lived it's hard to believe she would have shed a single tear for the regime that murdered her entire family. Douglas Murray touches briefly on the Trotskyist roots of neoconservatism, but goes into very little detail. Max Shachtman isn't even mentioned, a serious omission. That said, the anti-communist argument, which has its origins in Shachtman (and to a lesser extent Irving Kristol) is the most persuasive Murray has to offer. The Neocons were right about the cold war and they were right about Kosovo too. There can be no real argument there.

Murray's argument against the United Nations is powerful. He tells the amazing story of how, on November 10th 1975 the UN General Assembly passed (by seventy-two votes to thirty-five, with thirty-two abstentions) resolution 3379, which stated that "Zionism is a form of racism and racial discrimination". The motion was proposed by none other than the Ugandan dictator, Idi Amin. When he finished his speech Amin received a standing ovation. The following night, UN Secretary-General Kurt Waldheim, previously Oberleutnant Waldheum of the SA and a Nazi war criminal, threw a party in Amin's honour. Several times I have heard left-wing friends refer to this resolution. Not one of them bothered to mention that it was proposed by Idi Amin. No doubt it slipped their minds. Or perhaps they didn't know themselves and were simply repeating a line someone else had given them? Either way, thanks to Mr. Murray, I now have the truth.

Murray's argument against grandiose state sponsored 'anti-poverty' programmes is persuasive in parts. He quotes Irving Kristol to strong affect: "If you want to work with poor people, go out and work with poor people. I have great respect for people who do that. But when people start becoming bureaucrats of compassion and start making careers out of compassion—whether political, journalistic or public entertainment careers—then I must say I suspect their good faith." I have in my time known a few of the 'bureaucrats of compassion' Kristol refers to. They are, in my experience, among the most cynical people in the world. In practise they are always more concerned with preserving their own always well paid positions than they are in abolishing poverty. Of course it's in their interests to keep poverty going, because without poverty they would be out of a job. A few years ago a good friend of mine was on a government 'back to work' scheme here in Ireland. The supervisor was a former member of the pro-Soviet Sinn Fein-The Workers Party. But the actual workers, had no real rights. Wages cheques bounced. Those who complained about this were bullied into submission. Initiative was punished, talentless lackeys were promoted to management positions. One employee (a man) made a written complaint to the organisation's board about the fact that a member of the management team had on several occasions sexually harassed him. He was later pressurised into withdrawing this complaint by the board, which was of course full of the aforementioned lackeys. My friend says it reminded him of things he had read about the Soviet Union. But the supervisor could talk a good anti-poverty speech and was good at shaking politician's hands, when she wasn't on holiday in Russia, which she often was. Apparently she likes meeting Russian trades unionists. Giving money directly to the disadvantaged is one thing; I am all in favour of that. It is the one anti-poverty measure which actually seems to work. Giving it to bureaucrats who are meant to be acting in the interests of 'the poor' is often *profoundly* misguided.

The next time you hear a politician talk about his or her grand anti-poverty initiative, remember the story of my friend's 'back to work scheme' and the supervisor who likes meeting Russian trades unionists.

However Murray's general argument against welfare is rather one sided. He ignores the fact that at certain points in history interventionist government welfare programmes have proved crucial to the survival of the capitalist system. Without Roosevelt's New Deal, it's unlikely US capitalism could have avoided the chronic instability and political threats which plagued Europe in the thirties. This may be an inconvenient fact for neoconservatives, but it is nevertheless a fact. When he appears to argue for cuts in social welfare payments to the poorest, Murray comes across as heartless and, worse than that, impractical: "Benefit payments of all kinds must be recognized as a sop—a comprehensively wrong approach." What Murray fails to engage with is the fact that the "sop" of benefit payments mostly came into existence precisely in reaction to the crises of capitalism in the 1930s and the 1970s. It is not in the interests of anyone to have a significant proportion of the population starving and on the streets. Welfare stepped in where capitalism had temporarily failed. It is of course desirable that everyone should make use of their talents, and if at all possible pay their own way. But it isn't always realistic. This is one area in which Murray's youth and class background perhaps give him a somewhat narrow view: he is twenty-eight years old and a graduate of Magdalen College, Oxford. Murray has to date lived a relatively privileged life in a time of economic boom and near full-employment. In this context, it's not so surprising that he doesn't appear to really understand what the rough edge of poverty is like.

One of the problems with Murray's thesis, as it goes on, is that he tries to turn his version of neoconservatism into a totalising world view. This is one of the areas where we on the far Left went so wrong in the past. We always had to believe that our side was one hundred percent right and the other side one hundred percent wrong. This was how we justified everything from 'critical support for the Soviet Union' to the profound lack of internal democracy inside most far Left organisations, which were in effect miniature Stalinist states in the making. *If we are one hundred per cent right then how could anything we do ever be open to question?* This is how we thought. And it led us nowhere good. When he rails against the supposed mediocrity of "black culture", Murray sounds like an intolerant young fogey. The culture which gave us Miles Davis, Nikki Giovanni, Toni Morrison, Langston Hughes and Billy Holiday is surely at least as vibrant as the culture which gave us Andy Williams. And I say this as the proud owner of an *Andy Williams Greatest Hits* CD.

When he opposes state funding for Moslem schools but strongly supports giving government money to Christian and Jewish schools, he begins to sound like a knee jerk bigot. It may be a cliché, but one of the most impressive things about the USA is precisely its record of religious toleration. Tamper with this, and Bin Laden has won a significant victory. Murray's anti-immigration stance is similarly intemperate. "America", Murray argues, "does not want unstoppable immigration across its borders because it wants to remain America." He says it's no wonder the views of anti-immigrant Colorado Congressman, Tom Tancredo "are now being listened to, protective fencing around America's border and all." This sort of talk will most appeal to frightened little men, the sort who own lots of guns, vote for Pat Buchanan and think America had no business doing anything to help the Kosovo Albanians. It is not in keeping with the internationalism at the heart of most neoconservative thinking. And, another cliché perhaps, its ability to welcome and absorb immigrants is one of the reasons America has remained such a vibrant society, both economically and culturally. Tamper with this, and Bin Laden wins another round.

Murray is a staunch advocate of the war in Iraq. Many of his attacks on the anti-war side are effective. He tells us that George Galloway is a "friend of the Iraqi thug [and one time Foreign Minister] Tariq Aziz." This is of course true. He tells us that Galloway on one occasion told BBC *Newsnight* that: "the Iraqi Resistance does not target its own civilians." It comes as no surprise at all to me that Galloway would tell such an obvious lie. He tells us that, when asked in February 2004 if the anti-war movement should support the aforementioned Iraqi Resistance, John Pilger replied: "Yes…We cannot afford to be choosy." If this is true, and I have no reason to doubt it, given his own first hand experience as a journalist covering the results of the nutty tyranny of Pol Pot's Khmer Rouge, Pilger should have known that one always has to be 'choosy' about whom one supports. Otherwise one ends up being just as bad as the Western leaders, whom Pilger rightly criticised for cynically aiding the remnants of the Khmer Rouge in their guerrilla war against the then pro-Soviet Cambodian government during the 1980s. The enemy of your enemy is not always your friend.

What Murray—and it seems most neoconservatives— still fail to see is that noble intentions are not enough. There are plenty of crazy and thuggish dictators without whom the world would undoubtedly be a better place: Robert Mugabe, Kim Jong-il and President Islom Karimov of Uzbekistan, to name just three. I am all in favour of doing everything to isolate these three gentlemen, each of whom deserves the rope just as much as Saddam did. If I thought military intervention by the US would make the lives of people in Zimbabwe, North Korea, or Uzbekistan better, I would support it. If you can take a bully out, then you should take him out. But it has to be about actually making life for people in these countries better, not perfect, just better. This has clearly not been the case in Iraq. It has been four years. Too long. Too many lives. Both Iraqi and American. The situation in Iraq has proved to be utterly different from that in Kosovo, where intervention was welcomed by the Kosovo Albanians precisely because they did not perceive it to have been motivated by any selfish interest on the part of the US and Britain. Tony Blair was welcomed as a hero when he toured refugee camps in Kosovo. This will never happen in Iraq, because rightly or wrongly—at this stage it is immaterial— the majority of people in Iraq *do* believe that the US and Britain have conquest rather than freedom in mind for them. Iraq was occupied between 1919 and 1932 by the British under the 'British Mandate of Mesopotamia', sanctioned by that great protector of human rights and world peace, the League of Nations. Just as during the Vietnam War, the US was perceived by the majority of Vietnamese as attempting to continue where the defeated French colonialists had left off, the US and Britain are perceived by most Iraqis to be colonial invaders. What may have been the good intentions of some neoconservatives in the Bush Administration are, at this stage, irrelevant. We have to live in the real world. It's the only world we have. In *The Road to Wigan Pier* George Orwell wrote:

"Foreign oppression is a much more understandable evil than economic oppression. Thus in England we tamely admit to being robbed in order to keep half a million worthless idlers in luxury, but we would fight to the last man sooner than be ruled by Chinamen; similarly people who live on unearned dividends without a single qualm of conscience, see clearly enough that it is wrong to go and lord it in a foreign country where you are not wanted."

I have no doubt that Paul Wolfowitz and Richard Perle meant every word they said about wanting to bring democracy to Iraq. It was a noble and brave thing to want to do. But as a one time Left wing idealist I know that noble intentions on their own are useless. It's what actually happens that matters. It has been clear for some time that the US and Britain are not wanted in Iraq. It isn't working and it isn't going to work.

The very issue that made them famous, their idealistic push for regime change and democacy in Iraq, now threatens to confine the neoconservatives to the dustbin of history. Who will ever listen to them again? Since the end of the Cold War many Left wing groups have changed their names. It is perhaps time the neoconservatives considered doing the same. The worst thing, though, is that the ongoing failure of Operation Iraqi Freedom has perhaps fatally discredited the whole idea of taking military action to remove genocidal regimes. It will be a long time now before the international community (so-called) does anything about what is happening in Darfur. Many tens of thousands more will have to die.

Books In Canada, Summer 2007

The Poetry Reading Escapes From The Victorian Drawing Room

A poetry slam is a competition where poets recite their work, usually for three minutes each, sometimes without the aid of the page. What defines the genre is the foregrounding of performance. At the Cúirt Festival Grand Slam the judges are asked to consider the literary merit of the poem as well as the performance of the poet and the audience reaction. Some have argued that such overt competition is a bad thing. But having your poem (and the way you read it) judged by members of the audience is, surely, just another form of literary criticism. Yes, the wrong poem does sometimes win. However, the poetry reviews which appear in esteemed literary magazines are also on occasion wildly wrong. And as anyone who has navigated its sometimes shark infested waters will tell you: the Irish poetry scene was already a pretty competitive place, long before the poetry slam set foot here. In her essay 'Slams, Open Readings, and Dissident Traditions' Maria Damon argues that in America:

> slams have inaugurated some folks into a recent understanding of poetry as a competitive sport (a concept which makes traditionalists uneasy, in spite of the arguably more cutthroat competition for publication opportunities, admission to M.F.A programmes, and university teaching positions that poisons the mainstream "creative writing" community)

In Ireland the tradition of poetry, the spoken art is particularly strong. According to the Oxford Companion to Irish Literature:

> When Lady Gregory and Yeats were gathering folk material in Co. Galway in 1897 and thereafter, they encountered many stories about [Anthony] Reaftearaí (1779-1835) and found that his poems were still sung and recited.

Reaftearaí was illiterate, and his poems were never written down during his lifetime.

As the nineteen century moved on, Irish poetry found a home in the Victorian drawing room. Reaftearaí reciting his verses to peasant ne'er-do-wells gave way to Mister Yeats reciting his poems to small gatherings of old dears, and not-so-old dears, pausing between stanzas to sip tea from a bone china cup.

The worst contemporary readings, at which the poet reads to five or six people in a hotel with terrible carpet, have their roots in that Victorian drawing room. Although it has to be said, listening to Yeats's mannered recitation of his great poems in a grand setting was one thing; but sitting there, as A.N. Other mutters or declaims his or her latest to an almost non-existent audience, is a beast of an altogether inferior variety.

For the advocates of this sort of reading, the worst thing in the world would be if people had the temerity to turn up in significant numbers and actually appeared to be enjoying the experience. This would be poetry become entertainment, and must be stamped out at all costs, because, as we all learned at school, poetry isn't about entertainment, it's about suffering. To them, poetry readings are the literary equivalent of half eleven mass on a wet Sunday in Mullingar, without the jokes.

Lately what Dave Lordan calls "the live poetry movement" has energised the poetry reading scene by reconnecting Irish poetry with its own oral tradition. At the Over The Edge: Open Readings in Galway City Library, there are featured readers with an open-mic afterwards. It is not a poetry slam, or competition of any type. Many well known poets have been featured readers: the likes of Dennis O'Driscoll, Medbh McGuckian & Colette Bryce. But the democratic element which a properly structured open-mic introduces has been crucial to the event's success. Several poets who began at the open-mic have gone on to be featured readers. A similar openness is also crucial to poetry slams and other new reading series such as O'Bhéal in Cork and the White House readings in Limerick, both of which encompass an open-mic.

A feature of the recent development of the Galway poetry scene has been the central role of workshops. They are not the place to go if you have nothing to declare but your genius. Every word of every poem is open to question. The inclusiveness of the reading scene around Over The Edge and North Beach Poetry Nights is counter-balanced by the seriousness with which these workshops approach the task of helping emerging and beginner poets chisel their poems into the best possible shape. The idea that those who advocate the more populist approach to organising poetry readings believe, as one critic put it, "that all there's to it is to scribble down a mess of 'poetage' on a scrap of paper and yodel it out to an audience, and pretty soon you'll be up there with Paul Durcan and Rita Ann Higgins and Louis De Paor" is a caricature born out of ignorance.

Several poets, with a wide variety of reading and writing styles, have begun to emerge from this broad live poetry scene, of which slam is only a part. Poets such as Mary Madec, Neil McCarthy, Celeste Augé, Dave Lordan, Elaine Feeney, Ed Boyne, Noel Harrington, Mags Treanor, John Walsh, Micéal Kearney, Billy Ramsell and Lorna Shaughnessy.

The cliché performance poet—the might-have-been rock star in the leather-jacket, who instead of availing of the appropriate psychotherapy, leaps around the stage, making what sound like animal noises—does have some truth in it. I've met him. And I think I've met his brother. But in Ireland, he is not the norm.

Open readings are an import, yes, but so was the sonnet, imported as it was into English from Italy by Thomas Wyatt in the sixteenth century. Poetry is forever hybrid, never pure. The transformed poetry reading scene is helping Irish poetry finally shake off the legacy of that Victorian drawing room. And in the process will perhaps liberate us from what Dave Lordan, the Dublin-based winner of the 2005 Patrick Kavanagh Award & 2008 Strong Award, calls "the dictatorship of the one page lyric." There is a fork in the road. The sign going one way says 'Death in a provincial hotel', the sign going the other: 'New life'.

Poetry Ireland News (Nov-Dec 2006), *Vallum magazine* (Montreal, 2007) & *The Watchful Heart—A New Generation of Irish Poets* (Salmon Poetry, 2009. Ed. Joan McBreen)

The Condemned Apple

The Condemned Apple: Selected Poetry by Visar Zhiti, translated by Robert Elsie, and published by Green Integer, is quite simply the most disturbing collection of poetry I've ever read. Visar Zhiti was born on December 2nd 1952 in the port of Durres on the Adriatic coast. Between 1970 and 1973 his first published poems appeared in literary periodicals. By 1973 Visar was preparing his first collection of poems, "Rhapsody of the life of roses". Pretty standard stuff so far. If he'd lived in Ireland or Britain, Visar might have gone on to be nominated for a Forward Prize or some such, or been invited to showcase his first collection at The Ledbury Festival or Cúirt. Or he might have been ignored, and if this happened he would, no doubt, have complained about it to his friends. Such is the poet's life. At least as we have come to know it.

But Visar Zhiti didn't live in Brighton or Galway, he lived in a country under the absolute rule of the fanatical Stalinist, Enver Hoxha, who made Nicolae Ceausescu look like a benign liberal. Hoxha was a crank of gargantuan proportions. After first falling out with the Soviet Union, when Khrushchev admitted that Stalin had actually made a mistake or two, Hoxha then proceeded to fall out with the Chinese when, after Mao's death, they called a halt to the so called 'Cultural Revolution' and put the Gang of Four—including Mao's wife Jiang Qing—on trial. He condemned the Soviet Union, the People's Republic of China (and all their satellites from Cuba to North Korea) as "bourgeois revisionists". By the mid-nineteen seventies Albania had broken off diplomatic and economic contact with the rest of the communist world, it was now officially 'the only socialist country in the world'. It was also probably the second worst place in the world to live. In terms of grim Stalinist brutality, only Pol Pot outstrips the Albanian regime.

It was hardly the ideal circumstances in which to be publishing a first collection of poems. Zhiti had just submitted the manuscript of his first collection to the Naim Frasheri publishing company, when the 'Purge of the Liberals' happened at the Plenary Session of the Communist Party in Tirana. That the 'Liberals' in question only existed in Enver Hoxha's imagination was neither here nor there; they had to be purged anyway. And Zhiti suffered as a result. His work was interpreted as "blackening socialist reality". In 1979 two members of the League of Writers and Artists—their names are abbreviated here to R.V. and P.K—prepared an "expert opinion" on the poetic works of Visar Zhiti, at the request of the Ministry of the Interior. The two lackeys dutifully handed over their twelve-page 'expert opinion' to the authorities on October 24th 1979. Two weeks later Visar Zhiti was arrested. He was finally released on 28th January 1987, having done the rounds of the Albanian gulags, including the hellish copper mines at Spac.

This 'expert opinion' is republished in full at the back of the book. It makes chilling reading, in particular because its vehement denunciation of the "obscure language" and "hermetic" nature of some of Zhiti's poems reminds me of things I've actually heard socialist friends—some of them now former friends—say about the works of poets such as Medbh McGuckian and John Ashbery. Much left wing literary criticism, particularly as it appears in the small-press, is still laced with Stalinist attitudes. These days there are few overt Stalinists left, but there are certainly those on the literary left who talk Trotsky—'no party line when it come to art', and all that—but act Stalin when dealing with poetry which doesn't appear to serve the cause. Bad and all as things are, those of us who live in the Western world are at least still basically free to write whatever we want. Our poems may languish mostly ignored—that's a different issue—but at least Medbh McGuckian is not in danger of being denounced by the Ministry for the Interior for not being Adrian Mitchell or Linton Kwesi Johnson. Having condemned Visar Zhiti for the obscurity of some of his poems; R.V. and P.K of the League of Writers and Artists then go on to roundly condemn him for clearly saying what they don't want to hear:

"In the poem, 'For Julia', a mountain lass attends university wearing an old army jacket her brother gave her when he finished his military service. The writer's intentions are obvious here. In such poems he is endeavouring to blacken our life and make little of the economic well-being which socialism has brought to all of us, including the inhabitants of the mountains."

The major criticism I would have of this collection is that the offending poems, those referred to in R.V. and P.K's "expert opinion", are not included. It would have been very interesting to read them. The collection is dominated by poems Visar Zhiti 'wrote' during his years in prison. Deprived of writing paper and pencils, he memorised these poems in an attempt to avoid losing his mind. In the translation from the original Albanian to English, much must have been lost. And yet Robert Elsie's translations of Zhiti's poems are powerful and moving. Some of Zhiti's short poems are beautifully accurate, the sharpest perhaps being 'Moments Pass':

Moments pass
Over my body
Like lice

In this hole of a prison
Filled with the soil of suffering
I sit and wait

How sad it is
To be a warrior
         without war
(1982)

In the incredibly stark poem 'The Prison Shower Room', memorised while he was in Qafe-Bari prison camp in July 1983, Zhiti shows how even in the most dreadful circumstances human beings will cling to what small pleasures they can access:

The beloved water licks me with its tongue,
Soothing me all over.
The shadow of barbed wire,
Like a tattoo on a slave,
Stretches sombre on my skin
And I wash and wash,
And fall into another reality.

In the title poem Zhiti is clinging to his humanity by the barest thread "I, gone mad, scream in silence: / Hi there, world! / You may have forgotten me, / but not I you." In a sense, because the regime fell in 1990; and Visar Zhiti finally got out of the gulag; this is a collection with a happy ending. The poet preserved his sanity, and prevailed. In 'The Tyrant's One-time Office Near Which I Work' he even gets to visit the office of his tormentor and—echoes of Hannah Arendt—finds it to be a duller place than he'd imagined: "No abyss of convictions. No gun barrels / Emerging from drawers / like the eyes of metal detectors. / I stood silent, pallid / As if just over a long illness." This collection of poems was born out of one man's worst nightmare come true. It is one of those rare books with the power to fundamentally alter the way the reader thinks about the world. Buy it and keep it close. It is the starkest illustration I've seen yet of how the high Socialist hopes of the early twentieth century degenerated into such sordid everyday tyranny.

nthposition.com, May 2006

Too obvious for his own good

Straight Left—A Journey Into Politics by RUAIRÍ QUINN

Once upon a time, in a land of dole queues, moving statues and rotten coffee, when he was Minister for Labour and I was a duffle-coated member of Galway West Labour Youth, hating Ruairí Quinn was one of my favourite pastimes. During the miserable years of the 1982-7 Fine Gael-Labour coalition, he seemed to epitomise everything that was wrong with the Irish Labour Party. He was the 'socialist' who could (and did) quote Marx out of one side of his mouth, while out of the other justifying the use of the army to break the 1986 Dublin Corporation refuse workers' strike. If the revolution the teenage me believed was on its way had come to pass, it would have been very bad news indeed for Ruairí Quinn. A friend of mine, also then a member of Galway West Labour Youth, once told me that he thought that, come the revolution, we should start Ruairí Quinn's re-education by making him clean the late lamented Eyre Square public toilets without the aid of a mop, bucket or pair of rubber gloves. I remember thinking that this was perhaps a bit soft. All that said, it's been years now since I've given Ruairí Quinn much thought. The therapy is working nicely. And with Pat 'work permit' Rabbitte opening his mouth as he has been lately, there are clearly other more immediately deserving cases crying out to be dealt with.

I opened this book determined to give Ruairí Quinn a chance, to let him state his case. I was determined that, however difficult it might be, I would listen to what he had to say. Also, it is absolutely possible to profoundly disagree with what someone is saying and at the same time admire the way they say it. To pretend otherwise is to take the first step down the sad path of literary Stalinism.

Margaret Thatcher, Ronald Reagan and Adolf Hitler (to name just three) all sometimes had an undeniable way with words. It was one of the things that made each of them, in their different ways, so disastrously effective. This is definitely not the case with Ruairí Quinn. As a writer, he is dull beyond belief. The entire book is written in a passionless, pedantic style. The chapter on the aforementioned 1982–7 coalition government limps to a conclusion with the sentence: "We were out of government and a general election was not far away." In terms of literary style, that's about as thrilling as it gets. Gore Vidal he is definitely not.

The practical achievement Quinn gets most excited about is the creation of the FÁS Community Employment scheme in January 1993 when he was Minister for Enterprise and Employment in the Fianna Fáil-Labour coalition: "Since its launch 250,000 people have participated in the scheme." There is no doubt that CE schemes are the backbone of many important social and community services around the country; but the only people who actually get full-time (and well paid) jobs from these schemes are the managers. There are no real trade union rights, because if scheme participants complain, they won't be kept on for the second year. Surely those who do essential work in Community Resource Centres and Citizen's Information Centres (to name just two) deserve better than this? As it is, CE schemes are often the place where failed trade union bureaucrats and retired party hatchetwomen go to administrate. But then, it's hardly surprising that Ruairí Quinn would be proud of a scheme whose ultimate beneficiaries are a few hundred professional form-fillers. It's the sort of thing every podgy social democrat's dreams are made of.

The worst thing about this book, though, is its shaky relationship with the basic facts of Quinn's own political career. In his account of the 1982–7 period, the 1986 divorce referendum is not mentioned. This omission is striking because Quinn was a member of the coalition which proposed it. And the introduction of divorce was meant to be the sort of progressive reform which justified Labour's participation in what turned out to be an extremely unpopular government. It was a crucial part of their strategy. Presumably, it isn't mentioned because its huge defeat (by 65 to 35 per cent) makes it an unpleasant fact, and Ruairí Quinn doesn't like unpleasant facts. He far prefers to spend page after page waxing unlyrical about what a great thing FÁS is. Also not mentioned is the same government's decision in August 1984 to halve the subsidies on essential food items such as milk and bread. This was announced on the August bank holiday weekend, at the height of the holiday season, and the coalition hoped no-one would notice. In reality, there was uproar, and from that day they faced certain electoral doom, though they managed to cling to office for another ghastly two and a half years.

Such obfuscation aside, even when it comes to basic retellings of events he was involved in, Quinn often gets it wrong. On page 181 he says that, when Michael O'Leary resigned as Labour leader and joined Fine Gael in late 1982, the voting in the leadership contest which followed was "two for Barry [Desmond] and thirteen for Dick [Spring]". This isn't true. The candidate opposing Dick Spring wasn't Barry Desmond but Michael D Higgins, and the result was twelve for Spring and two for Michael D. On page 175 he has the 1982 Dublin West by-election (a disaster for Labour) take place on the same day as the Galway East by-election in which they did reasonably well. This isn't true either. The said Dublin West by-election took place on 11 May 1982, while the Galway East by-election took place two months later in July. I remember this because the Sunday before the Galway East by-election, the Connacht football final took place in Tuam. I was there with my dad, and all the three main political leaders— Haughey, Fitzgerald and O'Leary—turned up to canvas the crowd afterwards. It was a beautiful day spoiled only by the sight of a small plane dragging a 'Vote Fine Gael' banner across the sky.

Ruairí Quinn is so in love with being able to say whatever he wants, his relationship with fact has been distorted to such an extent that he is probably incapable of telling you the time without factoring in some sort of lie. The more 'successful' Labour leaders, such as Dick Spring, Tony Blair and (perhaps) Pat Rabbitte, are usually part con-man, part believer in their own propaganda. Ruairí Quinn's ultimate weakness was that, when it came to it, even he couldn't believe a word he said. As a political charlatan, he was just a little too obvious for his own good.

Red Banner magazine, March 2006

Odd Couple

My review copy of *Arthur & George* arrived on the morning of Monday, October 10th. The winner of the 2005 Man Booker Prize, for which *Arthur & George* was short-listed, was to be announced that night. It was the third time a Julian Barnes novel had made the list; *Flaubert's Parrot* got there in 1984, as did *England, England* in 1998. The publicity sheet accompanying the book announced, "*Arthur & George* is the odds-on favourite to win this year's Man Booker Prize." It seemed Julian Barnes's moment was at hand. At 11 pm I tuned in to BBC 2 to watch the station's live coverage of the awards ceremony at London's Guildhall. Despite the book's much trumpeted hot favourite status, it wasn't to be. The surprise winner: John Banville's *The Sea*. As I watched the ceremony, and listened to the literary equivalent of post-match analysis, it struck me that however successful a writer becomes-and with both critical kudos and a dedicated readership, Julian Barnes is about as successful a novelist as it's possible to be-there will always be those annoying near miss nights. The Booker Prize ceremony and the annual Galway County Council New Poet of the Year prize-giving evening have more in common than I had previously imagined.

Arthur & George is a fictionalised account of the relationship between Arthur Conan Doyle, the aggressive, eccentric creator of Sherlock Holmes, and George Edalji, the rather pedantic son of an Indian-born Church of England vicar, who instilled in his offspring a desperate wish to be accepted as more English than the English themselves. George's mother is English; she is the niece of the previous vicar, Compson. The residents of Great Wyrley aren't quite ready for this dark skinned vicar and his mixed-race family. And however much George goes on about England being "the beating heart of the Empire", that isn't about to change.

The novel moves in mostly short chapters, alternately titled

"Arthur" and "George", from the two boys' childhoods into their adult lives, and on to the point at which the two men's lives become briefly intertwined. Over a period of years, George's family is victimised by means of a series of poison pen letters and other increasingly elaborate dirty tricks. The letters include death threats against the young George. "I swear by God that I will murder George Edalji soon," the writer says on one occasion. I know I shouldn't say it, but Julian Barnes's detailing of the dirty tricks sometimes made the schoolboy prankster in me laugh out loud:

> "a young red-blooded curate from Norfolk [is] impatient to know why his fellow servant in Christ has summoned him all the way to Staffordshire on a matter of spiritual urgency, perhaps requiring an exorcism . . . Quantities of goods-fifty linen napkins, twelve young pear trees, a baron of beef, fifteen gallons of black paint-are delivered and have to be sent back. Advertisements appear in newspapers offering the Vicarage for rent at such a low price there is an abundance of takers. Stabling facilities are offered; so is horse manure . . . The following day a bailiff arrives to distrain goods in favour of an imaginary debt. Later, a dressmaker from Stafford comes to measure [his child sister] Maud for her wedding dress . . . In the midst of this scene, five oilskin jackets arrive for George."

The Reverend Edalji contacts the local constabulary, but the police do nothing, preferring the theory that the perpetrator is in fact George. Accused of sending death threats to himself, George's Kafkaesque journey begins. It ends with him being falsely convicted, as an adult, for killing cattle at Wyrley, and sentenced to seven years of penal servitude. George is eventually released on license, at which point the famous and wealthy author, Arthur Conan Doyle, becomes his champion. George Edalji's name is cleared, and the Court of Criminal Appeal is set up to avoid such miscarriages of justice in the future. For a time George is something of a celebrity. He is invited to Conan Doyle's wedding, where he feels slightly out place. Julian Barnes is a master of small ironies. His portrayal of Conan Doyle's involvement in the Edalji case is a perfect piece of understated satire on the particular egotism of celebrities-from Vanessa Redgrave to Bob Geldof—who involve themselves in helping the world's unfortunates.

In the early chapters there is a dichotomy between the prim

Anglicanism of George's family and the rather lackadaisical Catholicism of Arthur's. By page seven Barnes has George thinking, "he would prefer to stay here, inside, with Mother, with his brother Horace and new sister Maud, until it is time for him to go to heaven and meet Great-Uncle Compson," while Arthur's family are "always moving: half a dozen times in Arthur's first ten years. The flats seem to get smaller as the family grew larger." There is an even starker dichotomy, though, between how English society views George's mixed-race background and how it views Arthur's. Despite his desperate efforts to assimilate, George will never be allowed to be English. To be or not to be English is a question more easily resolved for Arthur: "Irish by ancestry, Scottish by birth, instructed in the faith of Rome by Dutch Jesuits, Arthur became English."

George's wish to be an Englishman does result in his acquisition of one quintessential middle-class English trait: a polite snobbishness which remains with him for the rest of his life. When his father tells him that he shouldn't look down on the farm boys who attend the same school as him, George doesn't really buy his father's explanation:

> "'Blessed are the meek, George. You know the verse.'
> 'Yes, Father.'"

But something in George resists this conclusion. He does not think Harry Boam and Arthur Aram are meek. Nor can he believe it to be part of God's eternal plan for His creation that Harry Boam and Arthur Aram shall end up inheriting the earth . . . They are just smelly farm boys, after all."

Throughout his life George Edalji maintains this Tory attitude toward the lower orders, even though he himself had been the victim of vicious prejudice. He quietly resents the fact that after taking up his case, Arthur Conan Doyle moves on to champion the cause of one Oscar Slater, who has been wrongly accused of murder. Slater is "a very low sort, a professional criminal", and though George accepts that he is not guilty of the murder in question, it bothers him to have to constantly listen to his own name being mentioned in the same breath as Slater's.

Arthur Conan Doyle's active belief in spiritualists, mediums and seances is wickedly and hilariously lampooned in the last section of the book. George sees an advertisement in the *Daily Herald* for a "Great Meeting" of 6,000 spiritualists to say goodbye to Conan

Doyle, who died a few days before. His family, including his wife, will be in attendance. They will sit on a stage, where one chair will be left empty for the spirit of Arthur Conan Doyle to occupy, should it so wish: "Lady Conan Doyle . . . asked that there be a demonstration of clairvoyance in the course of the evening. This would be performed by Mrs. Estelle Roberts, who had always been Sir Arthur's favourite medium." Despite his scepticism about such things, George decides to go along. Barnes's description of this scene in the novel's final thirty pages is the dramatic high point. Barnes manages both to poke savage fun at the spiritualists and to sympathetically examine the psychological roots of such things- our need to maintain a connection with those loved ones who have passed on. Julian Barnes is a hugely intelligent writer, whose beautiful wit is always humanely applied; *Arthur & George* is a great story masterfully told. If Jane Austen's spirit lurks anywhere, it is surely somewhere around his writing desk.

Books In Canada, December 2005

KGB Criticism

Director's Cut by DAVID SOLWAY

This collection of essays and reviews is, in effect, David Solway's personal manifesto in which he caustically, and sometimes hilariously, draws attention to everything he thinks is wrong with contemporary Canadian literature. Although *Director's Cut* deals with both fiction and poetry, Solway tends to skim the surface of recent Canadian fiction, telling us rather baldly in the preface that Ondaatje's *The English Patient*, Atwood's *The Blind Assassin* and Martel's *The Life of Pi* are 'among the most boring novels ever written and published in this country.' However, when it comes to what is clearly, for him, the particularly vexed question of contemporary Canadian poetry, Solway goes into far more forensic and damning detail. Where other critics would dodge this issue, Solway nails his banner starkly to the mast, when he says, again in the preface, that those twin demons—university creative writing departments, 'factories of undeviating blandness', and Canadian literature's heavy reliance on state subsidies—have over the past over the past two or three decades conspired to produce

> ...*a coterie of underachieving overproducers...That is why I am ready to challenge the literary hegemony of what we might call the Big Four— Al Purdy, Margaret Atwood, Ondaatje and Anne Carson—all of whom I contend are writers of such inferior quality that in a truly literate society they would be recognised as a national embarrassment.*

In Solway's view, 'although many readers...are growing heartily tired of this galaxy of plodders breveted above their proper rank, we are on the whole far too nice, too politically correct and, in a word, too "Canadian" to register our disapproval bluntly.' He acknowledges that such an open attack on received literary wisdom is a risky venture: 'it may lead to the standard critical mantra of "biliousness" and "negativity" or to charges of self-righteousness, presumption and pontifical imperiousness of temper.' He even concedes that 'there may be some truth to such an impeachment for no one can escape the penumbra of one's unconscious.' Then, having factored such risks openly into the equation, Solway launches his attack.

His first target, in a piece titled 'The Colour of Literature', is political correctness. This essay was sparked off by an article by George Elliott Clarke in the *National Post*. Clarke apparently argued (or at least appeared to be operating under the assumption) that literature is colour specific, and can be neatly divided into 'black-authored' and 'white-authored' texts. He also, it seems, went on to argue that a book such as *To Kill A Mocking Bird* is objectionable because it is 'more about white guilt than about black oppression.' Solway barks back that 'the history of white guilt is at least as important as the history of black oppression.' Now, while this is perhaps bending the stick a little too far, could the guilt of the relatively privileged ever really be 'at least as important' as the oppression on which their privileges were based? Later in the same essay, Solway demolishes the arguments of those on the PC left, who claim that it is wrong for writers to 'appropriate' the experiences of those from other class or racial backgrounds for the purposes of literature, by turning their own argument decisively back against them:

> Would it not have been a shame if the black woman poet Patricia Smith had been prevented by our new colour demagogues from writing in the persona of a white male supremacist, thus depriving us of an insightful poem like 'Skinhead', which accurately reveals the prejudices and self-justifications of the profoundly alien?

I have to say that whenever I read a critique of political correctness by a middle-aged white male, such as Solway, there always lurks in my mind the suspicion that while he typically thinks black people, women and gays should be more laid back about words such as 'nigger', 'bitch' and 'queer', he himself would no doubt immediately phone the police if some passing neighbourhood children yelled 'silly old fart' at him, while he was mowing the lawn. Middle-aged males are often very good at prescribing medicine for others, but very bad at taking it themselves. However, Solway puts this suspicion to bed in a way that is impressively forthright:

> Like Clarke, I too derive from a persecuted people [Solway is Jewish]...
> But neither I nor my parents ever objected to Shakespeare's cunning
> Shylock, a fixture on the curriculum...the fact that Shakespeare wasn't
> Jewish didn't bother us for a moment and, indeed, we could detect a
> quality of mercy in our noblest writer which complexified poor Shylock
> and even established a case for him.

So, in his opposition to political correctness in literature, Solway does not ask of anyone else anything he has not already asked of himself. As he sees it, imaginative writing is not a political act: 'The writer's tools and the way he or she uses them are far more important than the writer's conscious ideas or the writer's obvious identity. Thus Blake could say that Milton, who wrote best when he wrote of Hell, was of the Devil's party without knowing it.' On this point at least Solway is spot on; whatever one's political standpoint, books cannot be neatly divided into the politically righteous and the politically suspect, because the best books speak to different readers on different levels. Literature is a realm where the issue is not for the most part which side one is on politically. This is why Marxists (or at least the more broad-minded among those few who remain) can appreciate the poetry of a Welsh Anglican priest such as R.S. Thomas or a supporter of Margaret Thatcher such as Philip Larkin, while neo-conservatives can enjoy the work of that well known homosexual troublemaker, Walt Whitman.

'The Trouble with Annie' is an effective, if overlong, attempt to demolish the literary reputation of Canada's biggest poetry star of recent years, Anne Carson, whose verse novella *The Beauty of The Husband* won the T.S. Eliot award in 2002. Solway makes it clear that there's nothing personal about this: 'For what it's worth, I do not consider Carson a ghostly mutant skull witch, only a very ordinary writer of lenten inspiration who looked the wrong way.' He is less interested in humiliating Carson than he is in taking her admirers to task: 'As Christopher Hitchens contends with respect to Mother Teresa in *The Missionary Position*, the argument is not so much with the deceiver as the deceived: "If Mother Teresa is the adored subject of many credulous and uncritical observers, then the blame is not hers, or hers alone. In the gradual manufacturing

of an illusion, the conjurer is only the instrument of the audience".'
And it has to be said that the case Solway presents against Anne
Carson and her admirers appears, from this distance, to be a
compelling one.

In 'Standard Average Canadian', Solway does another demolition
job, this time on Al Purdy, a poet I have heard described as 'the
Canadian Charles Bukowski'. In the preface Solway cattily
complains about the fact the *International Herald Tribune* saw fit to
devote a column to Purdy's passing, when he died in April 2000,
'as if he were a figure of any real significance'. The problem with
this sort of jibe is that it always backfires on its author, tending to
make the open-minded reader a little suspicious about his motives.
If the issue is poetry, then why not talk about that rather than take
the easy option of kicking a guy when he's dead? However,
Solway's critique of Purdy's work is strong:

only Purdy

>   *surrounded by a dozen fierce Eskimo dogs*
>   *with an inexplicable (to me) appetite*
>   *for human excrement...*

*could turn a pack of huskies snapping at the squatter's hind-parts into
material for 'poetry'.*

Although, here Solway is more nuanced than in his essay on Carson;
he openly acknowledges that Purdy did also write a few decent
poems: 'Every failure has a flash of genius.' Whereas Solway is more
disturbed by the Carson's advocates than by the poet herself, the
source of his annoyance with Al Purdy is less his work than his
imitators:

>   *From the early seventies on, owing to Purdy's gathering influence,*
>   *Canadian poetry began to sound and look increasingly generic, as if,*
>   *despite whatever differences in specific content might be found in the*
>   *work of individual poets, the writing was being done by consortium.*

From what I've seen of it, though, contemporary Canadian poetry
is rather less under Purdy's influence than David Solway imagines.
Throughout *Director's Cut* a pronounced tendency towards over-
statement damages the case Solway is trying to make. At times, as

in the essay on Carson, Solway keeps going long after the argument has been won. At its most extreme, this reminded me of the recent case of a Romanian woman living in Dublin who was 'having some trouble' with her husband, and so asked some male Russian friends (who happened to be former members of the KGB) to have a word with him. They came around and beat him savagely with iron bars for five and a half hours. After the first hour, the man was probably already dead. But they kept beating him anyway. Like these gentlemen, Solway sometimes simply doesn't know when to stop. There is only so much bile readers can swallow without the doubt being planted in the minds of some that Solway is perhaps as much an embittered curmudgeon as he is a courageous iconoclast. And this is a real pity, because unlike many literary critics, he so often asks the right questions.

That said, his short essay 'Acorn, Lemm and Ojibway' a review of Richard Lemm's biography, *Milton Acorn: In Love and Anger*—is full of the sort of human warmth and nuance that Solway's detractors would no doubt think him incapable of. His account of hearing Milton Acorn read at the Café Bistro on Mountain Street, Montreal, in the early 1960s is as moving as it is hilarious:

> ...it is Milton Acorn I remember most vividly, giving his nightly oracular recitations, stomping up and down among the tables bellowing poems like 'I Shout Love' in a voice that can only be described as megaphonic. On one unforgettable night...as I sat shyly and inconspicuously in the smokiest corner, Acorn—as burly a poet as they came—suddenly grabbed me by the arm, dragged me upstairs to his shambles of a room and flung me on the bed where I cringed in a paroxysm of terror. Then he took a sheaf of poems from his worktable and without any preamble began to read them aloud, pacing back and forth, pausing only to light a cigar. This went on for about half an hour...when I had realised I wasn't about to be raped or murdered, I was able to concentrate somewhat on the poetry, which I found at the time entirely incomprehensible.

In this essay Solway allows himself to be [almost] a naïve enthusiast once again; the axe wielding critic of other essays is, for once, mostly absent. This is not to say that he is uncritical of Acorn's work, but the tone is very different. Perhaps if Anne Carson had once dragged the sixteen-year-old Solway upstairs, he would now be able to allow her similar leeway:

Acorn wrote a hit-and-miss kind of poetry: when he was off, he was embarrassing, but when he was on, the rightness of diction, phrase, line and cadence—the words following the contour of his speaking voice— and the importance of his subject revealed a master at work.

Director's Cut concludes with a sixty page extended essay into which many of the ideas in Solway's other essays are synthesised. His central argument is that Canadian poetry (and indeed most poetry) has now lapsed into either the banality of so-called common speech (Al Purdy) or self-indulgent obscurity (Anne Carson and Jorie Graham). Solway is particularly scathing about Fusion poetry, 'that frenzied and self-promoting balderdash', and 'the current spate of anti-war or anti-American poetry...It is [protest] of the permissible variety, an expression of popular sentiment that runs no risks and merely reinforces a broad status quo...rather than opposing it.' Though many of his arguments are well and wittily made, Solway in the end comes across as a man a little too fond of his own complaints. And then he poses the question: '...can one frankly conceive of any intelligent middlebrow reader spending an evening with Jorie Graham or Anne Carson in the way that my neighbour, a retired engineer, reads Housman and Hardy and listens to recordings of Dylan Thomas?' The problem with this is that by judging poetry on the strength of its likely appeal to retired engineers, Solway is ultimately adopting a backward looking reactionary stance. Yes, most contemporary poetry will no doubt vanish without making the slightest impression on the non-specialist reader. Hasn't this always been the case? But some of it will stick around. And there is plenty of evidence that posterity is more than capable of cutting inflated reputations down to size. Witness the recent critical collapse of the once very hyped Stephen Spender. Tomorrow will deal more ruthlessly with the hype of today than an army of David Solways ever could. And in shaping the poetry of tomorrow, we have to hope that the developing hunger for poetry of some sixteen-year-old, perhaps tonight attending his or her first reading in a café somewhere in Canada, will be at least as important as the opinions of Solway's retired engineer.

Canadian Notes & Queries, Autumn 2005

The Fringes of Power:
Downing Street Diaries 1939-55

John Colville, who died in 1987, was a diplomat and civil servant of-to put it mildly-the old high Tory variety. His description of his family background in the preface to this revised edition of his diaries is guaranteed to make egalitarians sneer: "My father and mother both came from well known and by no means indigent families, but they were younger children and therefore, thanks to primogeniture [the right of the eldest son to inherit his parents' property] comparatively poor. I say comparatively, for in the twenty years between the two world wars we wanted for none of life's essentials, always had six or seven domestic servants, owned a fleet of small boats in the Isle of Wight and had a house in one of London's less fashionable squares..." So, when Orwell was detailing the reality of life for the most downtrodden of the Many in *The Road To Wigan Pier* (and the hunger marchers were leaving Jarrow in England's depression-stricken North East for the long trek to London), young Colville was busy making do as a comparatively poor member of the same country's privileged Few.

After coming down (i.e. graduating) from Trinity College, Cambridge in 1936, Colville sat the entrance exam for the Diplomatic Service and in September 1937 began work at the Foreign Office, where he was allotted to the Eastern Department. At first, the young Colville was nowhere near the centre of the political and diplomatic action. When the world almost went to war over Czechoslovakia in September 1938, he was busy with the decidedly secondary task of trying to persuade unwilling British Army supply departments to provide guns for Turkey and Persia in competition with German and Italian offers:

"In those last days of September 1938, trenches were dug in Hyde Park, plans were made to evacuate schoolchildren, gas-masks were prepared for distribution and every young man I knew, not already a soldier or sailor, joined a "Supplementary Reserve". However, after the signing of the Munich Agreement Neville Chamberlain assured us that there would be peace in our time; and he really believed it."

Within a few months it became clear that the 'practical' gentlemen-politician advocates of appeasement, such as Prime Minister Chamberlain and his Foreign Secretary Lord Halifax, were fantasists of the worst order. On March 15th, 1939, Hitler, contrary to his solemn promises at Munich, ordered the German Army to seize Prague and, shortly afterwards, Danzig. On Good Friday Mussolini invaded Albania and Hitler began menacing Poland. Then, on August 22nd the Soviet and Nazi Foreign Ministers, Molotov and Ribbentrop, signed a non-aggression pact, agreeing to partition Poland between them and hand the Baltic states over to Russia. War was on its way. Colville had been due to sail to New York on August 23rd, for a month-long holiday with some Anglo-American friends on a ranch in Wyoming, when Hitler interrupted his late summer getaway plans. Unsure of what to do next, Colville decided to begin keeping a diary. One month later he was seconded from the Foreign Office to work at Number 10 Downing Street, then still occupied by the politically damaged Chamberlain. History and accident had conspired to put twenty-four-year-old John Colville at the very centre of things at the most crucial time. Wartime regulations forbade the keeping of diaries by civil servants, but this Colville thankfully ignored, making entries most days, and each night meticulously locking his diary away.

From such a tentative beginning, the diary grew into the immense document under review here. It stretches all the way from the collapse of 'Peace In Our Time' to the Suez Crisis. The latter is an event seen by many as the point at which Britain ceased to be an independent world power, and assumed its new role-one which has become the foreign policy orthodoxy for every Conservative and Labour government since-as a permanent ally (for better or for worse) of the United States. The world as it was when Colville first opened his diary and began to write on Sunday, September 10th, 1939, had vanished forever by the time he penned his 'Postscript To Suez' on April 7th, 1957.

Most cinematic portrayals of the Second World War—with rare exceptions such as *Casablanca*—tend to lull us into the belief that the outcome was never in serious doubt. Such a presentation of the Second World War amounts to a serious falsification of history. A Nazi victory may have been unthinkable. However, from the piled skulls of Cambodia to the sight of jets being deliberately driven into skyscrapers on an otherwise ordinary New York morning, there is plenty of evidence that the unthinkable is sometimes what actually happens. Just because we cannot imagine Germany emerging post-war, not flattened by bombs from the air and invading armies, but as the dominant military, political and economic power in the world, doesn't mean that that outcome hadn't been possible.

One of the best things about Colville's diaries is the way they undermine precisely that sort of complacency. On Thursday, June 20th, 1940-with France collapsing, the British Army humiliated in Norway, and Denmark, Holland, Belgium, Luxembourg, Poland and Czechoslovakia all invaded by the Germans-Colville wrote: "Heavy air-raids last night in which Southampton, Yorkshire and South Wales seem to have suffered. I suppose the real armada will come soon, troop carriers and all." At this stage Britain stood absolutely alone; the German attack on Russia was still a whole year away, and it would be another eighteen months before the United States, then still committed to isolationism, entered the war. A German invasion of Britain, which would almost certainly have succeeded, seemed imminent.

Colville's diary entries raise the important issue of the role of the individual personality in a time of crisis. On Wednesday, June 12th, 1940, he writes: "The news today is darker than it has yet been. General Haining says Paris will almost certainly fall within the next forty-eight hours. The French, although fighting with grim determination, are at the end of their tether, and although Reynaud [who succeeded Daladier as French Prime Minister two months before the German invasion] wishes to fight to the end, Petain is willing to make peace. He is worse than Bazaine in 1870 [the French Marshal who, during the Franco-Prussian War, surrendered the fortress of Metz with 173,000 men without putting up a fight]." Later, in a long entry written on the same day, Colville notes "Reynaud is as indomitable as Petain is defeatist." Of course, as his subsequent role in the collaborationist Vichy regime made clear, underlying Marshal Petain's 'defeatism' was something altogether more sinister.

It is valid to speculate that if Britain had also been invaded, the

Nazis would probably have found similarly willing British 'defeatists' to administer on their behalf.

A big point in Colville's favour is that, though some explanatory notes were added before the diaries were published, the diaries themselves are not at all self-serving. On Sunday October 1st, 1940, he says of Churchill [who joined Chamberlain's cabinet on September 3rd, 1939] after listening to one of his speeches: "He certainly gives one confidence and will, I suspect, be Prime Minister before this war is over. Nevertheless, judging from his record of untrustworthiness and instability, he may, in that case, lead us into the most dangerous paths." Here, Colville appears to go along with the appeasement era view that Churchill was reckless and that those more 'measured', like Chamberlain and Halifax, provided a necessary counterbalance. Like many of his class at the onset of the war, he seems not to have yet grasped that it was Chamberlain and his supporters who were leading Britain down the most dangerous path.

The quality which made Churchill a vital wartime leader was precisely his ability to see the world in the starkest black and white, and then take the necessary risks. Though he was an Establishment man to the core, and had a deep hostility to Socialism and Communism, Churchill was a single issue politician rather than a strict right-wing ideologue of the Thatcher variety. Like the Roman senator who began every speech with the words:
"Carthago Est Delenda" (Carthage must be destroyed), his career, both during his wilderness years and as Prime Minister, was dominated by one issue above all others. On Saturday June 21st, 1941, in reply to an after dinner question from Colville about why he, the arch anti-communist, was now willing to come to the aid of Russia, Churchill said that he had "only one single purpose-the destruction of Hitler-and his life was much simplified thereby. If Hitler invaded Hell he would at least make a favourable reference to the Devil." The following day Colville noted: "The P.M's view was that Russia was now at war; innocent peasants were being slaughtered; and we should forget about Soviet systems and the Comintern and extend our hand to fellow human beings in distress." It is hard to imagine Mrs. Thatcher saying, as Churchill did on Tuesday September 5th, 1944, that "if...there was a great left-wing majority [in the election after the war], let it be so: What is good enough for the English people, is good enough for me." Of course, that 'great left-wing majority' did indeed come to pass in

1945, and Churchill was swept from office immediately after winning the war, although he did return to Number 10 Downing Street in 1951, when, in another display of ideological flexibility, his Conservative Government left in place Labour's National Health Service and cradle-to-grave Welfare State. Colville's entertaining and informative diaries confirm Churchill as a politician who, unlike so many practical gentlemen of his day, was strong enough to abandon the pragmatism with which he typically approached politics. His confrontation with Hitler was a battle in which there were no shades of grey, only day on the one side and night on the other.

Books In Canada, September 2005

Nordkraft

Nordkraft is the first novel by young Danish writer Jakob Ejersbo, who already has a collection of short stories, *Superego*, to his credit. *Nordkraft* is translated into English by Don Bartlett. The glossy back cover is peppered with what, at first glance, looks like over-the-top praise from various reviewers in Ejersbo's native land. According to one, *Nordkraft* "is so gripping and strangely exhilarating because it brings to light linguistic inventiveness and a devil-may-care power to survive right down to the zero point of human existence." According to another, the novel deserves "6 stars out of a possible 6." Now, we all know how this sort of thing works. Back cover quotes are cherry-picked from the mixed bag of positive and negative reviews the vast majority of books receive. Nevertheless, there was something about the tone of these—and the sullen/ groovy photograph of the tattooed author which also appears on the back cover—that made me rather wary of this book, before I had even read a single word.

However, when I opened *Nordkraft* and actually began to read it, such world-weary suspicions were soon enough dispelled. The other novel it most resembles is *Trainspotting*, the 1993 best-seller by Irvine Welsh about the antics of a group of Scottish heroin addict friends. The big difference between them is that *Nordkraft* is by far the superior book. Whereas Irvine Welsh's characters never amount to very much more than hilariously amusing cartoon characters, Ejersbo's characters are all fully three dimensional people, who have entirely believable relationships with each other.

The story begins dramatically: twenty-one-year-old Maria has been sent by her drug-dealer boyfriend Asger to buy some cannabis in Copenhagen. (The couple live and do business in Aalborg, a small town in Northern Jutland.) Asger has assured Maria that there will be no police around the club where she is to buy the drugs. But there is a police raid, and a riot ensues. Maria ends up being cornered by a police dog:

> "The dog handler takes a step forward, the Alsatian rears up and lodges its paws on my shoulders, the dog's jaws snap at my neck. Someone screams. It is me...Nielsen [the dog-handler] approaches. With a hysterical scream I rip open my jeans. I catch a glimpse of her wide-open eyes as I thrust my hands down into my underpants. I grab hold; pull out the blood-soaked sanitary pad and hurl it at the dog which starts chewing it."

From there on the reader is drawn into the world of Maria, Asger and their friends: 'Loser', whose nickname tells us pretty much everything we need to know about him; Hossein, a drug dealing deserter from the Iranian Army to whom Maria is attracted; and Ulla with whom Maria briefly experiments in lesbianism. The novel is divided into three sections. The first, "Junkie Dogs", is mostly the aforementioned story of Maria and Asger. The second, "The Bridge", is about the return of Allan who had left Aalborg to work on an oil tanker travelling between Lagos and Rotterdam, in the hope that this might enable him to escape the old life. The final section, "The Funeral", tells the fragmented and often manic story of how they all gather for the funeral of their old friend, Steso. All this no doubt makes *Nordkraft* sound like just another sensational novel about young people taking drugs and dying, the sort of book destined to become a Hollywood film starring whoever the next Mickey O'Rourke happens to be. What saves it are Ejersbo's psychological insights. By far the most complex character in *Nordkraft* is Maria. Ejersbo's portrayal of Maria's relationship with her mother, from whom she is estranged, shows that he has a good understanding of the subtleties surrounding such small human dramas. Maria receives a note from her mother which reads:

Dear Maria,
I am very sorry for what I said about your father [her parents are divorced] Sorry, sorry, sorry, darling. Won't you call me? Then perhaps we could arrange a meal together? I hate it when we fall out.
Lots of love,
your mother.

Maria's response is predictable: "When we...fall out. We fell out bloody years ago. The cow runs my father down and then she thinks it can be sorted out with three sorrys and a kilo of warmed up frozen food." The way Maria sees the 'fall out' with her mother as final and irreparable (remember, she is only twenty-one years old) is typical of the stark either/or world view many early twenty-somethings try to impose on their lives, in order to mount some sort of resistance to the plans their parents and society have devised for them. By the time we're forty most of us come to realise that each of us has at least as many grey areas and hypocrisies as our parents ever did, and so we begin to view the human beings they were a little less harshly. But here Maria is too busy storming the barricades against the 'bourgeois' life her ex-hippy mother has in mind for her to bother with such nuanced reappraisals. She particularly despises her mother's new boyfriend, Hans-Jorgen, who is the head stage designer at the local theatre:

"He loves her flabby femininity, her caresses and devotion. He loves screwing with her and drinking wine and going to concerts with the Symphony Orchestra and taking city breaks in Barcelona and the whole shit. The only snag with my mother is me-the little brat who doesn't want to be a nice girl."

While Maria doesn't like to hear her still-hippy father criticised by her ex-hippy mother, her own description of him is one of the funniest passages in a book in which the humour has, thankfully, survived translation:

"My father worked as a roadie round Europe for all sorts of semi-known bands, but he only worked when the stars were in the right constellation... 'But we really need the money', my mother said to him... 'I can't go away now. The moon is in the perfect position', he said. The vegetable garden was weeded in strict accordance with Steiner's theories about the moon. And we had a dog, Mr. Brown, who refused to eat meat—he was a diehard vegetarian. If we gave him white rice instead of natural brown rice, he grumbled."

Many pages later, her relationship with the ineffectual Asger now over, Maria's life has narrowed to a few starkly posed choices: "Here she is sitting on the steps of the railway station, smoking herself silly on pot and having to choose between moving in with her overprotective mother, travelling out to her alcoholic father's or going down on her knees to a dishy but shady Iranian war refugee [Hossein] who carries a gun and wants her."

Though many of her friends go under, Maria survives and decisively leaves this life behind "to look for a job." We aren't told how she gets on, but her character is one who'll typically succeed, where many others fail. *Nordkraft* is a truly enjoyable read, far more than just another book about contemporary drug culture. It is a penetrating study of the way youthful rebellion often vanishes down the saddest cul-de-sacs, and a graphic illustration of the fact that however one might think one can resist it, society always has its way in the end.

Books In Canada, April 2005

Street ballet of the deaf and dumb
Everyday life in the GDR

Stasiland: Stories From Behind The Berlin Wall by Anna Funder

This study of life in the German Democratic Republic might at first glance be dismissed as an attempt by a writer-tourist from a relatively comfortable liberal democracy—Funder is Australian—to finish off something that was already dead. Given that everyone this side of North Korea knows the GDR was a miserable police state and that its end was ignominious, what more could there be to say about how ghastly life there was?

Funder's fascination with the GDR was sparked by a visit to Leipzig in 1994: "East Germany still felt like a secret walled-in garden, a place lost in time. It wouldn't have surprised me if things tasted differently here—apples like pears, say, or wine like blood." She begins her quest with a visit to Runde Ecke, the Stasi museum, the building that had previously housed the East German Ministry for State Security. The citizens' committee administering the museum had left all the desks just as they were the night the demonstrators took the building: "frighteningly neat". There were mounted displays on particleboard screens:

> My favourites were the pictures of protestors occupying the building on 4 December 1989... As they entered the building, the Stasi guards had asked to see the demonstrators' identity cards, in a strange parody of the control they were, at that very moment, losing. The demonstrators, in shock, obediently pulled their cards from their wallets. Then they seized the building.

Given its subject matter *Stasiland* could easily have become, in the hands of a lesser writer, a worthy but grim effort with a core readership of insomniacs who specialise in dead Stalinist states. But from the outset, Funder's acute awareness of the absurdity that often accompanies the worst tyrannies saves the book from that. In the museum she finds the following instructions to Stasi agents:

SIGNALS FOR OBSERVATION
1. Watch out! Subject is coming
—touch nose with hand or handkerchief
2. Subject is moving on, going further, or overtaking
—stroke hair with hand, or raise hat briefly
3. Subject standing still
—lay one hand against back, or on stomach
4. Observing Agent wishes to terminate observation because cover threatened
—bend and retie shoelaces
5. Subject returning
—both hands against back, or on stomach
6. Observing Agent wishes to speak with Team Leader or other Observing Agents
—take out briefcase or equivalent and examine contents

From this she conjures a blackly comic scene, made all the more laughable by the fact that this was supposedly being done in the name of world socialism: "I pictured the street ballet of the deaf and dumb: agents signalling to each other from corner to corner: stroking noses, tummies, backs and hair, tying and untying shoelaces, lifting their hats to strangers and rifling through papers." Funder's curiosity about this spy-dominated society (one full-time Stasi officer for every 63 people) is made all the more acute by her perception that many Germans, particularly those in the West, seem determined to forget it. A work colleague of hers at the overseas television service in what was West Berlin tells her in an outburst: "No-one here is interested—they were backward and they were broke, and the whole Stasi thing... It's sort of embarrassing."

What really makes this book work is the way Funder leaves, or at least appears to leave, any preconceived ideas she may have had at the door, and allows the people she meets—both victims and supporters of the old regime—to speak. The other piece of writing her open approach and deadpan style most calls to mind is Joan Didion's masterpiece essay 'Slouching Towards Bethlehem'. If someone is condemned, then they are condemned mostly by their own words.

One of the most exotic characters here is Karl Eduard von Schnitzler, whose job as presenter of the Black Channel in the GDR was "to show extracts from western television broadcast into the GDR—anything from news items to game shows to *Dallas*—and rip it to shreds". Funder interviews von Schnitzler and finds him still ranting in the glib, self-righteous way fallen-down apologists for horrible regimes often do. She reads him a long and very bombastic extract from a transcript of one of his broadcasts, which concludes with him saying that the Berlin Wall was "a service to humanity"! But in von Schnitzler's mind he has nothing whatsoever to be sorry about.

> When I finish, he's staring at me, chin up. 'And your question, young lady?'
> 'My question is whether today you are of the same view about the Wall as something humane, and the killings on the border an act of peace.'
> He raises his free arm, inhales and screams, 'More! Than! Ever!'
> He brings his fist down.

Like most demagogues, he's a great believer in exclamation marks. Later, von Schnitzler refers to Erich Mielke, Minister of State Security from 1957 until the regime's demise, as "a living example of the most humane human being". When he passed away to his eternal reward in 1999, most of those who'd lived under Mielke's ever watchful eye begged to differ, and the newspaper headlines read: "Most hated man now dead." As the closest thing the German Democratic Republic ever had to a television critic, it's perhaps not surprising that von Schnitzler finds time for a rant about the reality TV show *Big Brother*. However, even when he's taking easy potshots at such 'decadent', 'bourgeois' targets, von Schnitzler manages to make western capitalist society at its most Martha Stewart/Britney Spears venal seem infinitely preferable to his socialist workers' republic.

The tragedy is that he believes every word of his finger-wagging defence of the GDR. Unlike many younger regime apparatchiks, von Schnitzler didn't originally join the Communist movement out of a wish to make a soft living spying on and brainwashing his neighbours: "von Schnitzler is one... whose ideas were moulded in the 1920s by the battle against the gross free market injustices of the Weimar Republic and then the outrages of fascism".

Of course, once a political (or religious) movement has convinced itself that it—and it alone—has all of the answers to humanity's problems, then the telling of politically convenient lies and the demonisation of opponents does tend to become institutionalised. And so the lies multiply until the organisation in question (in this case East Germany's ruling Socialist Unity Party) has, at best, a semi-detached relationship with reality. If people are afraid to tell you the truth, then you'll never hear it—which is not to say that you'll escape it, as Stalin's children, from Honecker to Ceaucescu, all eventually found out.

Perhaps the saddest story here is that of Miriam from Leipzig and her husband Charlie. Her story begins in 1968, when "the old University Church was demolished suddenly, without any public consultation". A demonstration against the demolition was doused by the police with fire-hoses and arrests were made. Miriam, then sixteen, and her friend Ursula decided "this was not right" and so proceeded to stick up some leaflets which simply said "Consultation, not water cannon!" and "People of the People's Republic speak up!" This one impetuous teenage act resulted in an eighteen-month prison sentence in Stauberg, the women's prison at Hoheneck. After prison Miriam says that she was "basically no longer human". Over the next ten years there followed an unsuccessful attempt to scale the Wall, and then the beating to death in custody of her husband, which the Stasi went to elaborate lengths to pass off as a suicide. Miriam's story, beautifully written by Funder, is well worth the cover price on its own. It is also a stark reminder that, however much some of us on the left may still find it galling to admit, when US presidents and others stood on the western side of the Berlin Wall and talked about 'liberty' and 'freedom', those words did actually mean something.

Books In Canada, October 2004 & *Red Banner* magazine, December 2005

Twenty years ago today

GB84 by DAVID PEACE

This time twenty years ago the miners' strike was raging across the water. The morning radio news was full of flying pickets and pitched battles between miners and police; the evening television dominated by images of the same. Names of places such as Cortonwood, Ollerton and Orgreave were burned into the consciousness forever, simply because we heard them so often. Cortonwood, where it all started when the National Coal Board announced the Yorkshire pit's arbitrary closure in the first week of March 1984. (Within days it became clear that this was part of a much larger pit closure programme.) Ollerton, the Nottinghamshire mining village where the strike claimed its first fatality, when a young miner was killed in a crush between pickets and police during the second week of the strike. Orgreave, the Yorkshire coking plant then vital to Britain's electricity supply, where the miners tried to repeat their famous 1972 victory, when they succeeded in closing down a similar plant at Saltley, Birmingham by mass picketing. This time it didn't work.

The miners were lured to Orgreave from South Wales, Kent, Durham, Yorkshire, Scotland and elsewhere in their tens of thousands on a beautiful June day to face the massed power of the British state: thousands of police with horses, dogs and riot gear, ready willing and able to turn the miners back. From that day on we all knew something had changed. This wasn't 1972 or '74. There'd be no easy victory. And in the end, which didn't come until March 1985—a whole year after the strike started—there was no victory at all. The miners went back without a settlement, their union's power broken, their industry about to be destroyed.

David Peace's novel GB84, which he describes as "a fiction,

based on fact", charts the course of the strike from the optimism of the early days through the pitched battles of the summer to the slowly dawning reality of total defeat. Peace uses a traditional, linear narrative structure interspersed with extracts from the diaries of two miners, Martin and Peter. And much of the time it works. Younger readers for whom it has only ever been ancient history would certainly get at least an idea what the miners' strike was like. Peace writes in an accessible style, without in any sense trying to dumb complex issues down. And he provides us with more than the bare documentary facts. Indeed, GB84 brings that apocalyptic year more credibly back to life than many an earnest but dead-in-the-mouth speech at many a far-left meeting. It makes the strike human again by giving the reader a real sense of the emotions it stirred, as the high hopes of activists and trade unionists everywhere turned so bitterly into their opposite.

GB84 is divided into five chapters, each of which has a title of its own; the first four—'Ninety-nine red balloons', 'Two Tribes', 'Careless Whisper' and 'There's a world outside your window and it's a world of dread and fear'—are all references to popular songs of the time. No doubt some will complain that Peace is trivialising such a momentous event by naming a chapter in a book about it after a song written by George Michael. I have to say, though, that for some strange reason I personally have always found it useful to know what was in the charts the year a particular event happened. Knowing, say for example, that T Rex were in the charts the year Ireland joined the EEC, or that Renee and Renato had their one hit wonder 'Save Your Love' the year the Falklands War happened, somehow makes those events seem more rather than less real. Sad, I know. But true. With the title of the last chapter 'Terminal, or the Triumph of the Will' Peace leaves such frivolity behind, and everything is suddenly deadly serious.

For me, the best writing in the whole novel are the two extracts from Martin's diary in the last chapter. On day 364 of the strike, when more than 50% of the miners have drifted back to work, and the National Executive of the NUM have voted by 98-91 to recommend a return to work without a settlement, Martin summons up the ghosts of all the previous generations of miners whose struggles made the tradition which Thatcher succeeded in decisively trampling into the dirt:

The Dead that carried us from far to near. Through the villages of the Damned, to stand beside us here. Under their banners and their badges. In their branches and their bands—Their muffled drums. Their muted pipes—That whisper. That echo—Their funeral marches. Their funeral music—That moans. That screams—Again and again. For ever more—As if they are marching their way up out of their graves. Here to mourn the new dead—The country deaf to their laments.

In many ways the tempo of *GB84* resembles that of a symphony, and the extract quoted above is part of its catastrophic crescendo. The black pessimism of the defeated strike is, in a sense, the flipside of the near hubris of its early days:

Motion to back strike is proposed. Motion is seconded. Motion is backed 100 per cent—Folk head off to Hotel or Club. Lot of talk about '72 and '74. I'm having a piss in Club when this bloke says to me, It'll be right then? I say, How do you mean? We'll win? He says. Yeah, I tell him. What you worried about?

Generally speaking, Peace weighs the significance of different events well. One criticism I would have, though, is that, in a couple of places, his narrative is laced with just a little too much fatalism. Clearly, by Christmas 1984 the miners were doomed. But between March and October it was by no means certain that Thatcher was going to prevail. Peace downplays the significance of Arthur Scargill's mistake in not calling a national ballot, by having one of his characters—an almost satanic government advisor referred to throughout the book as "the Jew"—talk in March 1984 about "the very unlikely event of a national ballot and… even unlikelier event of a vote for strike". Now, this is simply wrong.

All the evidence is that the overwhelming majority of miners and their families supported the strike at this stage. And, if anything, support for the strike increased during the spring and summer as more miners and their wives became more actively involved and the strike gained the sympathy of a wide coalition of people in every corner of Britain: everyone from traditional trade unionists to the Sikh community in Birmingham to gay and lesbian groups in London and Brighton. The miners received money collected by sympathisers worldwide, even receiving cheques from such non-proletarian sources as Elizabeth Taylor and the American billionaire John Paul Getty.

If there was a national ballot anytime between April and August, when 80% of miners were on strike, it's a racing certainty that the ballot would have endorsed the strike. And this would have given the strike added legitimacy, which would certainly have persuaded many of those in Nottinghamshire and elsewhere, who continued to work, to join the strike. The miners' tradition was to have a national ballot when the issue was national strike action: there were national ballots in both 1972 and 1974. And not to have had one in 1984 was a major strategic error brought about, at least in part, because of the top-down, bureaucratic socialism of miners' union president Arthur Scargill. The miners may still not have won if there'd been a ballot, but they would certainly have had a much better chance.

Another window of possibility David Peace downplays a little is the threatened strike action by NACODS, the union which represented pit deputies, who were responsible for pit safety, and without whom no mine could legally stay open. They voted to strike 82% to 18% in October 1984. If implemented this would have meant every working miner in Britain being sent home. After seven months the strike would finally (if only by default) be 100% solid. With a NACODS strike still threatened, Peace has the aforementioned government advisor 'the Jew' confidently ranting:

> there must be no further negotiations. There must be no further promises of no compulsory redundancies. There must be no amnesty and no jobs for any miners convicted of criminal offences. The times have changed…

At that stage outright victory was probably beyond the miners' grasp, but the likelihood has to be that, if NACODS walked out and stayed out, there would have been some sort of fudge. Thatcher would not have claimed her famous victory. And everyone would have lived to fight another day. However, the national executive of NACODS called off their strike at the last minute, and the rest is history.

Peace does a good job, though, of illustrating the sheer ruthlessness of the Thatcher government. On page 253 he has 'the Jew', whose actual name is Stephen Sweet, draw up a strategy to entice striking miners back to work:

The Jew wants a copy of the entire payroll for the National Coal Board. The Jew wants every miner's name checked against police and county court records—The Jew wants weaknesses—

Men who have transferred to their pit. Men who live a distance from their pit—Men who are married. Men divorced. Men who have children. Men who can't—Men who have mortgages. Men who have debts—Men who used to work a lot of overtime. Men who used to have a lot of money—Men who have weaknesses. *Age. Sex. Drink. Theft. Gambling. Money.* The Jew wants lists.

Two things really irritated me about this mostly enjoyable book. The first was the constant reference to this government advisor as 'the Jew'. Only a couple of times in 462 pages is he referred to as Stephen Sweet. I could see no reason for this, other than self-indulgence (or perhaps an attempt at sensationalism) on the part of the author. The second was the gangster sub-plot, which is so obviously a tacked-on afterthought (perhaps designed to widen the book's appeal?) that it's actually possible to read the rest of the book without bothering with the sub-plot at all.

So, *GB84* is an imperfect book rather than any sort of masterpiece. But it has enough going for it to make it worthwhile. And it obviously has particular significance for those on the left. It charts the progress of a battle, which in the words of Michael Eaton—the all too real Saatchi & Saatchi advisor appointed by Thatcher to advise the Coal Board—was the "decisive occasion in recent British history when the right won and the left lost". It took some on the left years to come to terms with the gravity of this defeat. When Thatcher resigned six years later, the bulk of her agenda had been carried out. The miners' strike was the decisive point when Thatcherism might have been stopped, but wasn't. Her victory ended a long period of heightened class conflict in Britain which had started with the struggle against the Heath Tory government in the early 1970s, and created in its place a world fit for New Labour and Michael O'Leary of Ryanair. It also allowed Thatcher to become a credible icon for those advocating the restoration of the free market in eastern Europe. From Poland to Dublin Airport the after-effects of the miners' defeat can still be seen. It was in a sense the event which, more than any other, gave birth to the world we all now live and work in.

Red Banner magazine, December 2004

An Arid Season

by MICHAEL D HIGGINS

An Arid Season is Michael D Higgins' third poetry collection. Its publication after the 11 year hiatus since his previous collection, *The Season Of Fire*, is certain to get both literary and political mouths chattering. Higgins' high profile as Labour Party spokesperson on Foreign Affairs and possible presidential candidate pretty much guarantee this will be one of those rare poetry books that everyone—from earnest young women with politically correct earrings to literary tweed jackets who've had one brandy too many—will feel it necessary to have some sort of opinion about.

The most common reaction though to Michael D's poetry is a kind of bemused bewilderment at the fact that it exists. Most people tend to think it somehow exotic or strange that here is an elected representative who, as well as asking Brian Cowen questions in the Dáil and holding clinics in the Atlanta Hotel on Saturday mornings, also writes poems. Many politicians, from Pat Rabbitte to Padraic Conneely, are performers, perhaps even artists of a sort. But when one thinks of them as a group, poetry is generally speaking not the first thing that comes to mind.

One of the difficulties Higgins has faced as a poet is the lack of real critical engagement with his work. Those who admire his politics—and they are many, especially among those in the arts—find it difficult to apply to his poetry the standard of criticism they would routinely apply to any other poet's work. The themes in this collection are a mix of the personal and the political. In 'Pol Pot In AnlonVeng', he deals with politics at its most surreal, taking us into the mad world of Pol Pot in a mostly understated poem in the course of which the architect of the killing fields chillingly announces that: "He is finished/He says/With politics."

In the personal poem 'Conversations' Michael D pleads with

his daughter Alice Mary that they should "Have conversations/ Instead of rows". In the overlong title poem 'An Arid Season' he talks in rather abstract and desolate terms about the "darkness" he sees on the political horizon; while in the short poem 'Nocturne 2' he nicely describes the quiet death of a moth: "Lonely in its last/Weak beat/Of Death."

His best poems are those, such as the excellent and disturbing two page narrative 'The Madman's Visitor', in which he avoids rhetoric and sticks to the images: "Past the fragrant nuns she moved/Defeating the cacophony of their metal bowls,/A symphony in duty/To the God/ For whom they starched their headresses/And sterilised their instruments." His weakest poems are those overwhelmed by rhetoric and abstraction. 'The Sense-Voices of Spirit' in eight short lines has the words spirit, grief, sorrow, time, space, and void, but not a single concrete image to help readers link these concepts and emotions to the tangible world of things we can touch, smell, or taste. Even if *An Arid Season* does, on balance, contain just a little more chaff than wheat, Michael D Higgins proves himself to be a poet of more range than most and there is certainly good poetry here. In 'Old Waders on Koh Samet' a poem inspired by his friend Paddy Leahy who went to spend the last of his life in Thailand, he beautifully expresses strong emotions in a quiet way. And in 'Revivalists' he proves himself capable of putting his sense of humour to good satirical use.

Galway Advertiser, August 5th, 2004

George Orwell:
Anything but a saint

This year's centenary of George Orwell's birth at Motihari in
Bengal, India on 25 June 1903 has seen a marked upturn in interest
in both his writing and in the man himself. Penguin have
republished pretty much everything he ever wrote—both novels
and non-fiction—in a series of glossy volumes, which basically add
up to a collected works. There have also been two new
biographies, both of which have, to varying degrees, tended to try
and shift the spotlight away from George Orwell the stubborn
teller of inconvenient political and social truths, and onto Eric
Blair the man behind the pseudonym. There is certainly something
to be said for this sort of approach: as someone who has read
Orwell's work voraciously over the years, I know that I certainly
relished the opportunity to leaf through the grubby details of his
life. But it also has its limitations.

The fact that he visited prostitutes, made throwaway comments
insulting gay contemporaries such as W H Auden and didn't like
Scottish people is, of course, on one level all very interesting. On
another level though, it is also completely irrelevant, doing nothing
to diminish his critiques of capitalism and Stalinism in works such
as *Homage to Catalonia*, *The Road to Wigan Pier*, *Animal Farm* and
Nineteen Eighty-Four. I once heard someone say that everything
Karl Marx had ever written could be dismissed as "rubbish"
because he had throughout his life failed to properly provide for
his family and (if that wasn't bad enough) then got his housekeeper
Helene Demuth pregnant. If we were to use, for example, the fact
that Orwell apparently sometimes paid for sex to try and in any
way diminish his achievement as a writer and political thinker,
then this is the rather intellectually limited road we'd be heading
down.

George Orwell was certainly flawed, both as a man and as a writer. When he came back to England in 1927, after a five year stint as a Colonial Policeman in Burma, and decided to 'become a writer' he looked like an unpromising wannabe indeed. The poet Ruth Pitter was a neighbour of his at the time:

> He wrote so badly. He had to teach himself writing. He was like a cow with a musket.... I remember one story that never saw the light of day... it began "Inside the park, the crocuses were out..." Oh dear, I'm afraid we did laugh, but we knew he was kind, because he was good to our old sick cat.

Like most fledgling writers he started off by writing reams of grandiose garbage. According to Bernard Crick's 1980 biography, *George Orwell: A Life*, the worst of this appears to have been a fragment of a play about a couple whose baby is dying because they can't afford an operation she desperately needs. Despite their desperate need for money Francis, the father, refuses a job writing

> advertising copy for "Pereira's Surefire Lung Balm"... because the firm are swindling crooks, the substance is noxious, and, besides, he's got his artistic integrity to consider. When his wife reminds him of Baby's needs, he suggests that for her to prostitute herself would be no worse than the job she wants him to take. Then the scenario turns abruptly from naturalism to expressionism... "Everything goes dark, there is a sound like roaring waters.... the furniture is removed"; and we are in a timeless prison cell, in something like the French Revolution, with POET, POET'S WIFE and CHRISTIAN who "sits... reading a large book. He has a placard inscribed DEAF around his neck."

If a contemporary version of this early Orwell lived around the corner from me, I have no doubt that I would spend a good deal of time desperately trying to avoid him. I have known such people, and they rarely grow up to produce masterpieces!

The early Orwell's politics were similarly unfocused and adolescent. Looking back on his earlier self from the vantage point of 1936 he has this to say in *The Road to Wigan Pier*:

> I wanted to submerge myself, to get right down among the oppressed; to be one of them against their tyrants. And, chiefly

because I had to think everything out in solitude, I had carried my hatred of oppression to extraordinary lengths. At that time [roughly 1928-1933] failure seemed to me to be the only virtue. Every suspicion of self-advancement, even to the extent of making a few hundreds a year, seemed to me spiritually ugly, a species of bullying.

The early Orwell's stance could in a sense be read as the oh so predictable, immature rejection of bourgeois society by one of its more privileged members, who almost certainly only had a vague notion of what the word 'bourgeois' actually meant, and certainly hadn't the faintest idea how things might actually be changed. Most such middle-class radicals end up being reabsorbed by the society they once supposedly despised. At best they become concerned journalists or perhaps panellists on *The View*. At worst they end their days thinking that Eoghan Harris has a point. But Orwell was clearly different. His rebellion was a serious one. It was this failure-worshipping stance that led Orwell to drift down among the tramps and winos of London and Paris. And from this milieu came the material for his first book *Down and Out in Paris and London*, published in 1933. By now his writing had greatly improved from those early, laughable efforts. The plain documentary prose style for which he became famous was already visible. Orwell was nothing if not persistent. In Ruth Pitter's words: "he had the gift, he had the courage, he had the persistence to go on in spite of failure, sickness, poverty, and opposition".

The three years that followed saw him produce a novel each year, *Burmese Days* (1934), *A Clergyman's Daughter* (1935) and *Keep the Aspidistra Flying* (1936). The most significant of these for us is probably Burmese Days, a damning anti-imperialist indictment of British colonial rule in Burma: something Orwell knew from the inside having spent five years working as a policeman for the British regime there. All of these novels deal with issues important to Orwell: repression, snobbery, hypocrisy, the worship of money and the frustration of artistic ambitions.

My personal favourite is *Keep the Aspidistra Flying*: his grim but often hilarious portrait of Gordon Comstock, a down-at-heel poet forever beset by financial embarrassment and sexual frustration. Comstock is obsessed with not being ruled by the "Money God", and so leaves a well-paying job writing slogans for an advertising agency, and gets a badly-paying job in a bookshop. At least that way he has some hope of retaining his integrity. In the end, though, his girlfriend Dorothy becomes pregnant, and Comstock leaves the bohemian life behind; surrendering himself entirely to a future of Money, Marriage and Aspidistra Plants, all the things he previously spat venom at. Orwell's portrait of Gordon Comstock is perhaps the last we see of his early, unfocussed radicalism. *Keep the Aspidistra Flying* was published in January 1936. By December of that year the Spanish civil war had broken out, and Orwell was in Barcelona fighting against the forces of General Franco as a member of the POUM militia.

Just after he'd finished *Keep the Aspidistra Flying* Orwell was commissioned by Victor Gollancz of the Stalinist-leaning Left Book Club to write a book of documentary non-fiction about the condition of the unemployed in the industrial north of England. Gollancz offered him an advance of £500, huge money for the time. This was the coincidence which finally pushed George Orwell to become the overtly political writer we have come to know. Years later his friend, Richard Rees, recalled: "There was such an extraordinary change both in his writing and, in a way also, in his attitude after he'd been to the North and written that book. I mean, it was almost as if there'd been a kind of fire smouldering in him all his life which suddenly broke into flame at that time."

Of course, events external to Orwell's day-to-day life played their part too. 1936 was the year when the political and economic crisis of the 1930s really began to seriously gather speed as it hurtled towards disaster and the second world war. In March of that year the German army moved into the previously demilitarised Rhineland: the first serious violation by Hitler of the Versailles Treaty. In May Italy invaded Abyssinia and Mussolini declared that a new Roman Empire had been established. In July General Franco's forces rose up and tried to overthrow the Republican government in Spain. When they didn't achieve the easy victory they'd expected, the Civil War began. In October Oswald Mosley's Blackshirts were beaten off the streets by anti-fascists at Cable Street as they tried to march through the predominantly Jewish areas of the East End of London. And in December the abdication of Edward VIII did its bit to heighten the sense of crisis.

When he asked Orwell to write the book that would become *The Road to Wigan Pier*, Victor Gollancz hoped Orwell would produce a book something like *Down and Out in Paris and London*, except that this time the focus would be industrial workers (both employed and unemployed) and their families, rather than tramps. What Orwell actually produced was a book of two very distinct halves: the first of which provides us with some of the best portraits to be found of working class life in 1930s England. For the first time Orwell begins to see working class people as human beings fully conscious of their own position at the bottom of society. He recalls watching a young woman trying to unblock a drain with a stick: "I thought how dreadful a destiny it was to be kneeling in the gutter in a back-alley in Wigan, in the bitter cold, prodding a stick up a blocked drain. At that moment she looked and caught my eye, and her expression was as desolate as I have ever seen; it struck me that she was thinking just the same thing I was." Elsewhere, though, his view of working class life is just a little sentimental:

> In a working-class home—I am not thinking at the moment of the unemployed, but of comparatively prosperous homes— you breath a warm, decent, deeply human atmosphere which is not so easy to find elsewhere.... on winter evenings when the fire glows in the open range and dances mirrored in the steel fender, when Father, in his shirt-sleeves, sits in the rocking chair at one side of the fire reading the racing finals, and Mother sits the other with her sewing, and the children with a pennorth of mint humbugs, and the dog lolls roasting himself on the mat.

The picture Orwell paints of this happy, simple life is so idyllic that it sounds almost like something from a speech by Ronald Reagan or Éamon de Valera. I have to confess that whenever I actually come across people as apparently wholesome as this, I tend to suspect that they either have bodies buried under the patio, or that Father (God bless him) will in the fullness of time be escorted into the back of a police van with a bag over his head, having been caught bouncing the little ones on his knee just a little too vigorously.

The second part of *The Road to Wigan Pier* is a hilarious, if at times slightly cranky portrayal of the organised left of the time. On his way to attend the Independent Labour Party Summer School at Letchworth, Orwell spots two other likely attenders:

both about sixty, both very short, pink and chubby, and both hatless. One of them was obscenely bald, the other had long grey hair bobbed in Lloyd George style. They were dressed in pistachio-coloured shirts and khaki shorts into which their huge bottoms were crammed so tightly that you could study every dimple. Their appearance created a mild stir of horror on the top of the bus. The man next to me, a commercial traveller I should say, glanced at me, and then, back at them again, and murmured, 'Socialists'.

Orwell seems to have enjoyed the company of those working-class activists he met in the North of England. But he quite clearly detested those on the left he saw as middle-class trendies or frauds of any type:

'Socialism' calls up, on the one hand, a picture of aeroplanes, tractors and huge glittering factories of glass and concrete; on the other, a picture of vegetarians with wilting beards, of Bolshevik commissars (half gangster, half gramophone), of earnest ladies in sandals, shock-haired Marxists chewing polysyllables, escaped Quakers, birth-control fanatics and Labour Party backstairs-crawlers. Socialism, at least in this island, does not smell any longer of revolution and the overthrow of tyrants; it smells of crankiness, machine-worship and the stupid cult of Russia. Unless you remove that smell, and very rapidly, Fascism may win.

Despite his scathing portrayal of much of the left, Orwell himself was nevertheless moving sharply to the left politically. In early December he put the finishing touches to *The Road to Wigan Pier* and made arrangements to travel to Spain, where the civil war was now raging. He arrived in Barcelona on 22 December and was greatly impressed by what he saw:

The Anarchists were still in virtual control of Catalonia and the revolution was still in full swing.... Practically every building of any size had been seized by the workers and was draped with red flags or with the red and black flags of the Anarchists... Every shop and café had an inscription saying that it had been collectivised; even the bootblacks had been collectivised and their boxes painted red and black. Waiters and shop-walkers looked you in the face and treated you as an equal. Servile and even ceremonial forms of speech had temporarily disappeared. Nobody said 'Se or' or 'Don' or even 'Usted'; everyone called everyone else 'Comrade' and 'Thou', and said 'Salud' instead of 'Buenos dias'.

His experience in Spain would lead Orwell to write what is arguably his best book, *Homage to Catalonia*. But during his time there, Orwell was more than merely another literary tourist: he fought and was shot and badly injured. It was Orwell's personal experience of the role played by the Stalinists in undermining and ultimately sabotaging this revolution that turned his fairly vague suspicions about 'the cult of Russia' into an implacable hostility towards Stalinism, which he retained for the rest of his life. During the Russian-backed crackdown on 'Trotsky-Fascist Fifth Columnists' in June 1937 he himself was forced to go on the run, sleeping rough on the streets of Barcelona for several nights, to avoid being rounded up because of his membership of the anti-Stalinist POUM militia. His friend George Kopp was imprisoned and tortured by the Stalinists. The torture with rats of Winston Smith in Room 101 in *Nineteen Eighty-Four* is apparently partly based on Kopp's treatment at their hands. And yet despite this tragic outcome Orwell left Spain inspired with an impatient, nagging hope:

> For months past we had been telling ourselves that 'when we get out of Spain' we would go somewhere beside the Mediterranean and be quiet for a little while and perhaps do a little fishing... It sounds like lunacy but the thing that both of us wanted was to be back in Spain. I have recorded some of the outward events, but I suppose I have failed to convey more than a little of what those months in Spain mean to me.... the mountain dawns stretching away into inconceivable distances, the frosty crackle of bullets, the roar and glare of bombs; the clear cold light of the Barcelona mornings, and the stamp of boots in the barrack yard, back in December when people still believed in the revolution...

I think it is fair to say that Orwell left Spain a convinced revolutionary socialist. Indeed he spent the next couple of years waiting for a revolution, which in the end didn't come. His next novel *Coming Up For Air* (1939) is a portrait of George Bowling, "a fat insurance salesman worn down by a loveless marriage, the expense of a family, children who despise him". Bowling is exactly the sort of beleaguered Mr Average that Orwell thought the left needed to appeal to if it was ever to successfully take power in Britain. The coalminers and the cranks would never be enough. A win on the horses inspires Bowling to leave home one day and try to recapture something of his youth:

> Of course, his journey is doomed—the small town [where Bowling grew up] had been engulfed by suburbia and his woodland paradise infested with fruit juice drinking, nudist vegetarians, and Garden City cranks.... Katie, his childhood sweetheart is now a worn-out, middle-aged drab and the secret pool, the symbolic centre of his childhood fantasy, turned into a rubbish dump. The horrors of the mass society have overwhelmed the holy places and Doomsday threatens in the form of Hitler, Stalin and their streamlined battalions.... George returns to his bourgeois prison to face again his nagging wife and unlovable children.

Orwell had clearly moved a long way since the days when he believed that salvation could only be found down among penniless tramps. He was now thinking in concrete terms about how society might actually be changed, and socialism made to appeal to both the working and middle classes.

The two novels that followed before his premature death from TB in 1950 are what transformed him from a medium-sized 1930s figure into a literary superstar, whose books will no doubt still be read two hundred years from now. *Animal Farm* (1945) is an ingenious Swiftian satire on the Russian Revolution betrayed. Orwell has been accused by some of jumping on the Cold War bandwagon, and of allowing his work to be used by reactionaries and warmongers to attack the socialism which he himself believed in. It's important to remember, though, that when Orwell was writing and trying to find a publisher for *Animal Farm*, the second world war was still on, and Britain, the United States and the Soviet Union were still allies. Orwell actually found it incredibly difficult to find a publisher for what was seen at the time as another trouble-making book by him. So the charge of opportunism really doesn't stick. The later film version famously removed the last scene in which the animals peer in the window at the pigs and the humans having dinner together, and cannot see any difference between them. Orwell's message that the Stalinist bureaucracy (represented by pigs) and the capitalist class (represented by the humans) were as bad as each other was no doubt a little inconvenient for the American cold war propagandists who hijacked his work. The manner in which life-long Soviet apparatchiks such as Boris Yeltsin and Vladimir Putin managed to transform themselves into advocates of the gangster capitalism now prevalent in Russia shows that he was of course right: in the last analysis there was very little difference between them and the capitalist class in the west. They would do anything to hang onto their positions, up to and including the complete restoration of capitalism.

His last major work was *Nineteen Eighty-Four*, a deeply pessimistic portrait of a totalitarian society, resembling those that then existed in eastern Europe. By the time he wrote this book, Orwell had moved away from the near Marxist stance of *Homage to Catalonia*. His revolutionary moment had passed. And of course world events had moved on too. The second world war was over, and Britain now had a Labour government which Orwell basically supported. It was this Labour government—a government far to the left of that of Tony Blair—which created the National Health Service and the welfare state. By the time Orwell died in 1950, the political situation was completely different to that of 1936, the year he went to fight in Spain. Orwell had an instinctive rather than a theoretical attitude to politics. His contempt for theoreticians—"shock-haired Marxists chewing polysyllables"—led him to spend a lot of time reacting against other people's ideas rather than coming up with credible ideas of his own.

The worst example of this is his stance in relation to World War II. In September 1938, during the Czechoslovakia crisis, Orwell published a short article in *New Leader*, the paper of the ILP, in which he stated: "We repudiate... all appeals to the people to support a war which would, in fact, maintain and extend imperialist possessions and interest, whatever the incidental occasion." At the time the Stalinist parties where promoting the Popular Front policy. 'Democracy not Fascism' was the slogan, and they were desperate to build an alliance against Nazi Germany between the Soviet Union and western powers, such as Britain and

France. When the war actually came both Orwell and the Stalinists did a complete about-turn. The Hitler-Stalin pact was signed and the Soviet Union stayed out of the war until it was attacked itself in 1941. The Communist Parties attacked the war as 'imperialist', just as Orwell had in his *New Leader* article. Orwell, on the other hand, strongly supported the war effort and vehemently attacked the anti-imperialist, anti-war point of view, which he himself had still supported as late as August 1939. He never properly explained this about-turn. A likely explanation is that, by then, his hatred of the Stalinists was so intense that when he heard them saying one thing, he would, if at all possible, say the opposite.

His hatred of all things Soviet was also his motivation when, on 2 May 1949, he sent a list of suspected Communists and fellow-travellers to the British intelligence services. The list included both literary figures such as Stephen Spender and J B Priestley, and left-wing Labour MPs such as Ian Mikardo and Tom Driberg. A number of the people named by Orwell were outed not just as suspected Communist sympathisers but also as homosexuals. Given that homosexual acts between men were still illegal in Britain, and would remain so for another twenty years, this was a particularly disgusting thing to have done. Orwell handed MI5 material which they would no doubt use to blackmail left-wingers and socialists. There is no excuse for this.

Despite his many faults, though, Orwell is a writer whose work will always be of interest to socialists, indeed to thinking people everywhere. Yes, he was often cranky, often wrong. But his dogged pursuit of some of the awkward questions of his time led him to produce two of the masterpieces of socialist literature, *Homage to Catalonia* and *Animal Farm*. And the bravery he showed in opposing Stalinism—not when it was weak and collapsing but at the height of its power—cannot be lightly dismissed. If this Orwell lived around the corner from me, he would be welcome to come around for a cup of tea anytime. No doubt we would argue. But such is life.

Red Banner magazine, June 2004

Poetry, Politics And Dorothy
Gone Horribly Astray

Almost every poet I know is prone to exaggerate the influence poetry can exert on world events. Maybe it's the cold reality of poetry's marginal position in society which leads many of us, particularly at a time of crisis like this, to talk in loud excited voices about how poetry can supposedly make politicians sit up and listen or even 'change the world'. This benign egocentricity is perhaps a necessary indulgence to save us from vanishing entirely into our garrets, or academia, convinced of the total irrelevance of what we do. If we don't at least convince ourselves that poetry can matter, then how on earth can we expect to convince anyone else?

The truth is poetry can sometimes play a role in actually changing people's minds, by convincing the reader (or listener) emotionally of an idea to which he or she may be intellectually opposed. If a poem can win the ideologically hostile reader's heart, then his or her head will surely follow. Such a heightened experience of poetry can lead to a transformed world view for the reader. So, yes, the influence of poetry can be profound.

However, the power of poetry is more elusive, less tangible than that exerted by politicians and generals. Yes, poems such as Wilfred Owen's *Dulce Et Decorum Est* and W.H. Auden's *September 1 1939* continue to exert power over readers all these decades later. But in his lifetime Wilfred Owen's poetry failed to shorten by a day the war that, in its last week, claimed his life. And for all its warnings, the glittering genius of Auden could do nothing to stall humanity's mad march to Auschwitz and Hiroshima. That's just not how it works. And despite our sometimes inflated sense of ourselves, deep down most of us know that, during his famous afternoon lie-downs, George W. Bush probably doesn't lose a moment's shut-eye worrying about people like us. One doesn't get to be President of the United

States, or President of anywhere, by caring what poets think.

Generally speaking, if the government does something of which we disapprove—such as sending back illegal immigrants, giving the police more powers, or cutting spending on the Arts—it is probably a measure their heartland constituency, in Kansas or the Home Counties, quietly approves of. The disaster that lurks around George W. Bush's bed these days—and must soon shake even him awake—is precisely the way opposition to his colonial adventure in Iraq has now worked its way into the heartland. (In Tony Blair's case the opposition to the war has long since captured the heartland; for him the argument is lost.)

In Galway on the West coast of Ireland, where I live, I have listened to everyone from the taxi driver to the postman to the old woman in the laundrette spit poison against George W. Bush. I spent my teenage years foaming at the mouth every time President Reagan appeared on television, while my American relatives loudly supported him. Last Sunday I had a telephone conversation with my uncle John, a retired construction foreman in Chicago, and he was angrier about Bush than the teenage me ever was about Reagan. The other week I spoke to my partner Susan's stepmother in Philadelphia; a woman, who has been very good to us over these last few years, but who also happens to be a gun owning, pro-death penalty registered Republican. She told me that in November, because of the war, she would be voting for "anyone but Bush". And, no, she wasn't just playing to the gallery of the pinko son-in-law-to-be. When it comes to politics this woman is more likely to invite you to an NRA convention, than she is to spare your feelings in such a soggy, sentimental way.

Paradoxically, the fact that opposition to the Iraq adventure is now so widespread has made writing poetry about it very difficult; poetry and consensus make bad bedfellows. At least that's been my experience. In the aftermath of 9/11 I found it easy enough to write poems about the attack on the Twin Towers, the War in Afghanistan etc. Lately I have found it impossible to address the Iraq issue in poetry. Back then one was taking a risk by saying anything about the War On Terror; and risk makes for good poetry. Now, all one is doing when one writes a straightforward anti-war poem is agreeing with the old woman in the launderette, and pretty much everyone else on the planet. When the whole world is saying the same thing the words get used up and jaded, and we start to sound like newscasters rather than poets.

Poets are often guilty of indulging in hyperbole when talking about political issues, but it is difficult to overstate the extent of the disaster now facing the Coalition in Iraq. In early 2003 the Bush/Blair arguments for war were: (1) Saddam Hussein had weapons of mass destruction which he would not hesitate to use against the West, Israel and his own people; (2) Saddam Hussein was a bloodthirsty despot who ruled by murder and torture; and (3) under Saddam Hussein, Iraq had become an operational base for al-Qaeda.

We now know that there were no weapons of mass destruction. This is something we tend to shrug off a little too easily. Just because we believed all along that Bush and Blair were lying about the existence of WMDs in Iraq does nothing to lessen the significance of the fact that every thinking person in both the US and Britain now knows for sure that their respective governments looked them in the eye in late 2002/early 2003 and told barefaced lies about such an important issue. In March 2003 most people in Britain believed Tony Blair was wrong about Iraq, but they certainly did not believe he was a ruthless liar. Now that truth is unavoidable. If this wasn't bad enough, the Blair government's attempts to coerce the BBC into covering the issue up is blamed by a large proportion of the British public for the suicide in Oxfordshire last summer of a softly spoken Government scientist, Dr David Kelly. There will be no coming back from that for Tony. Like a worn out animal, he'll stumble on a while longer, but must surely soon find a quiet place to politically die. Perhaps after the European elections. Perhaps a little later.

No one has ever argued that Saddam Hussein was anything but a bloodthirsty tyrant; I'm sure that's how he'd describe himself in the unlikely event of being asked for a resumé by a prospective employer. However, since the release of the photographs from Abu Ghraib prison, the problem for the US is it now seems that the difference between Saddam's regime and their occupying forces is less about fundamentals than it is about degree. Okay, so (as far as we know) the US army don't actually dissolve their opponents in acid-baths, as Saddam famously did. But they do force prisoners to strip, tie what looks like a green plastic bag over each prisoner's head, and then pile naked prisoners on top of each other like carcasses in an abattoir. Only these are human beings. And then they take photographs. The last people crazy enough to go out of their way to create such damning evidence of their own war crimes were the Khmer Rouge.

For me, the most bizarre photograph is one which shows Specialist Charles A. Graner of the US Army wearing a particularly silly smile and a pair of turquoise gloves, his arms folded as he gives the camera the thumbs up. In front of him stands Specialist Sabrina Harman. She is bending over, and smiling, looking for all the world like Dorothy from the *Wizard of Oz* gone horribly astray. Immediately in front of her are a pile of naked, hooded Iraqi prisoners.

At this point, I should say that if offered a choice between being dissolved in sulphuric acid and being stripped naked and forced to lie in a pile of similarly naked prisoners, I think I'd generally choose the latter. Life is almost always better than death. But it's not much of a choice. And it certainly has nothing at all to do with freedom or democracy. As British Conservative MP Boris Johnson has said: before these photographs, the Coalition could at least claim that, whatever else, political prisoners were no longer being tortured in Iraqi jails. Now that too has been lost. And like Tony Blair's integrity, it won't be coming back. From now on we can expect many more such photographs. Some will no doubt be hoaxes. But enough will turn out to be true.

The centre of Galway is now covered in posters for a rally to protest against George W. Bush's visit to Ireland on Saturday June 26th. The posters use a photograph of Private Lynndie England holding a dog leash at the end of which is a naked Iraqi prisoner, and the simple but superbly effective slogan "This Torturer Used Shannon Airport". The Irish Government's decision to allow US Military aircraft to refuel at Shannon has been a particular bone of contention here. I spotted at least three posters from which Lynndie England's face had been burned away with a cigarette. And from an apartment complex in Dominick Street, an American flag now hangs upside down. It is one of the Bush administration's outstanding achievements, that they have managed to turn the overwhelming pro-American sympathy that was the Irish reaction to the attack on the Twin Towers into this sort of bitter hostility. But their achievements don't end there.

The objective of the 'War On Terror' was supposed to be the defeat of al-Qaeda. In March 2003 the network was non-existent in Iraq. However, a few weeks ago the leader of their newly founded Iraqi section, Abu al-Zarqawi, beheaded Nick Berg, a 26 year-old businessman from Westchester, Pennsylvania, and broadcast the execution on the internet. Berg is heard to say "My name is

Nick Berg, my father's name is Michael, my mother's name is Suzanne. I have a brother and a sister. David and Sarah. I live in Philadelphia." Then the knife is ruthlessly applied. Berg's headless body was found on the outskirts of Baghdad. Nick Berg's father Michael was quoted as saying "Nicholas Berg died for the sins of George Bush and Donald Rumsfeld. The al-Qaeda people are probably just as bad as they are—but this administration did this." The whole situation is starting to look like a trap of al-Qaeda's making, into which America sleepwalked in the aftermath of 9/11. Wherever Osama Bin Laden is tonight, he must be laughing horribly into his beard.

There'll be no easy solutions here. Even if Kerry wins in November, Iraq will continue to crack into at least three pieces. And as long as American troops remain—and don't kid yourself, John Kerry certainly won't withdraw them—the more fundamentalist leaders will continue to gain support. Just as al-Qa-eda is not a liberation movement with whom the European or American left could ever make common cause, the Shia cleric Muktadr Al-Sadr is no Ho Chi Minh or Ché Guevara. What is opening up now in Iraq is a catastrophe.

And the world, from New York to Madrid to Bali, is wracked by a conflict between a Texan buffoon, who by his own admission can't be bothered to read the newspapers or listen to the television news, and a batty Saudi aristocrat out to restore the seventh-century Islamic Caliphate, which at its zenith stretched from the Persian Gulf to Spain. Not a good situation. As activists and writers, the best we can do for now is avoid parroting pretend solutions—the last thing the world needs to hear is more untruths, even well meaning ones—and bear witness as honestly and as well as we possibly can, be it in poetry or be it in prose.

nthposition.com, June 2004

Mentioning the war

101 Poems Against War.
Edited by MATHEW HOLLIS and PAUL KEEGAN

100 Poets Against the War.
Edited by TODD SWIFT

Irish Writers Against War.
Edited by CONOR KOSTICK and KATHERINE MOORE.

During these past few years I have written and read more articles and essays than I care to remember about the relationship between literature and politics. But despite the sound and fury the subject has generated, it was until recently a debate which appeared to be going nowhere fast. At the end of the day one was always left dealing with two determinedly separate worlds. One with its precious poets and monstrous literary egos. The other with its dry slogans and Party line. However, the lead-up to the war in Iraq saw all that change as radicalism came dramatically back into fashion, with a sudden resurgence in politically motivated writing and publishing. The books reviewed here are just three of those which resulted. Similar anthologies of American and Canadian anti-war writing are now also available on amazon.com.

The most striking difference between these three books is that while both *Irish Writers Against War* and *100 Poets Against the War* both specifically protest against the recent war with Iraq, Faber and Faber's *101 Poems Against War* is aimed less at that war in particular than at 'war' in general. This has to be a weakness, because everyone (or almost everyone) is against war in general. Indeed, to be against war in the abstract is so easy as to be almost meaningless. The other weakness of the Faber & Faber book is that most of the poets included in it are dead—the Chinese poet Li Po having shuffled off this mortal coil as long ago as the year 762. So it would be harsh indeed to criticise them for having nothing to say about Bush and Rumsfeld!

There are, though, several excellent poems among Faber's *101 Poems Against War*. Many, such as Wilfred Owen's 'Dulce et Decorum Est', W H Auden's 'September 1, 1939' and Keith Douglas's 'How to Kill', are already widely available. Others, such as Carl Sandburg's 'Grass' were new to me. The clunker of the collection is without doubt Harold Pinter's 'American Football (A Reflection upon the Gulf War)':

Hallelujah!
It works.
We blew the shit out of them.

We blew the shit right back up their own ass
And out their fucking ears...

Now this might be (in the narrowest sense) on the right side politically. But that shouldn't stop us from recognising it for what it is: a shoddy piece of literary laziness which (sorry about this, Harold) should never have seen the light of day. If someone turned up at my local writers' group and read a poem such as this, I would probably spend the following week quietly hoping they never came back.

At the opposite end of the spectrum, the poem I most enjoyed was Hayden Carruth's 'On Being Asked to Write a Poem Against the War in Vietnam':

Well I have and in fact
more than one and I'll
tell you this too

I wrote one against
Algeria that nightmare
and another against

Korea and another
against the one
I was in

and I don't remember
how many against
the three

when I was a boy
Abyssinia Spain and
Harlan County

and not one breath
was restored
to one

shattered throat
mans womans or childs
not one not

one
but death went on and on
never looking aside

except now and then
with a furtive half-smile
to make sure I was noticing.

The fact that the author clearly understands the powerlessness
of poetry in the face of the onward march of politics and war
makes his poem/protest all the more effective. For me the image
of death "never looking aside / except now and then / with a
furtive half-smile / to make sure I was noticing" is far more
arresting, more disturbing than anything in the Harold Pinter rant
quoted earlier. For those of you just becoming interested in poetry,
101 Poems Against War is worth a read. There is good stuff here.
It's just that whereas the other two books at least promise
something new, it seems from the outset to basically offer us more
of the same.

SALT Publishing's *100 Poets Against The War* is an anthology of
a very different political colour indeed. Firstly, all the poets
published in it are alive and kicking, indeed some of them are still
relatively young. Secondly, it is a specific protest against the recent
war with Iraq. It originated as an e-book published on the
London-based web-magazine nthposition.com. Its editor, Todd

Swift, put out a call for anti-war poems on Monday 20 January. Within a few days he had received over one thousand poems by e-mail from poets worldwide. And the following Monday—the day of Hans Blix's first weapons inspection report to the UN—*100 Poets Against The War* was born as an e-book which could be downloaded and printed off from a variety of websites worldwide. New editions appeared on subsequent Mondays. At the time of writing the various internet versions of *100 Poets Against The War* have been downloaded more than 70,000 times. It has, by any standards, been a stunning success.

Much of this is down to its editor, the Paris-based Canadian poet Todd Swift, who is without doubt one of the most dynamic figures in the poetry-publishing world at the moment. The version published by SALT contains most, though not all, of the poems published in the various e-books. The largest group of contributing poets come, interestingly enough, from the United States. Indeed, my pick of the entire anthology is a prose-poem written by Richard Peabody, an American poet based in Arlington, Virginia. His 'Dubya Anabasis' takes an ironic look at how George W Bush will be remembered, post-World War III:

> The son of the 41st President (George Herbert Walker Bush) Dubya is thought now to have been a puppet of his father's staff. He disappeared in the fallout following the vaporisation of Washington, DC. For years it was claimed that he died in a bunker in West Virginia, or was hiding in caves in Texas or Argentina... Dubya appears briefly as a Taniwha in Keri Waratah's rock opera Whiro, he is presented as a bland puritanical man of relentless torpor, the "child is father to the man" who gradually mutates into a mythical demon...

Peabody's admittedly outrageous satire seems to me to be closer to the mark than the sort of po-faced over-earnestness which so often plagues politically engaged poetry. Another poem I enjoyed was British poet Sean O'Brien's 'Ballad':

> Here we go to war, boys—
> Rally round the flag.
> Tony cleans it up, boys—
> He's the oily rag.

Tony talks in sentences
And even paragraphs:
When Dubya tries a speech act
Half the planet laughs.

Wonder what's at stake, boys?
Why we're off to war?
Someone on the take, or
Was that the time before?...

100 Poets Against The War is one of the most innovative poetry-publishing projects of recent years. It contains a glittering variety of poems, from ballads such as the one quoted above to poems of the more elusive Language Poetry variety: Swift is clearly an open-minded editor indeed. It is also the only one of these three books which is truly international, including work by poets from Canada, the United States, Australia, France, India, Britain and, of course, Ireland.

Irish Writers Against War edited by Conor Kostick and Katherine Moore is, in one sense, the most overtly political of the three anthologies. Towards the back of the book there is 'A Note on the Irish Anti-War Movement' by Richard Boyd Barrett. And while royalties from *100 Poets Against The War* go to Amnesty International, any royalties from *Irish Writers Against War* go directly to the Irish Anti-War Movement. The most distinctive thing, though, about *Irish Writers Against War* is the fact that it contains within its covers not just poetry but also journalism, short stories and extracts from novels. Many of the contributors such as Roddy Doyle, Brendan Kennelly and Seamus Heaney are very famous. However, others are much less well known, and the editors are to be congratulated for putting together a lively little anthology which is anything but a collection of the same tired old names.

There are a couple of really excellent short stories: the disturbing 'Tear-duct Capacity' by Cork-based writer Kevin Doyle, and the beautiful 'The Meadow' by Susan Knight. Of the poems I most liked Pat Jordan's 'After War', Sinéad Morrissey's 'The Wound Man' and Mark Granier's 'When'. However, the best pieces of writing here are probably the journalistic pieces. Terry Eagleton's 'What Is Fundamentalism?' is top class both in terms of form and content: he both knows what he's talking about and knows how best to say it. A rare combination indeed.

Fundamentalists, however, fail to realise that the phrase 'sacred text' is self-contradictory. Since writing is meaning which can be handled by anybody, any time, it is always profane and promiscuous. Meaning which has been written down is bound to be unhygienic. Words which can only ever mean one thing would not be words. Fundamentalism is the paranoid condition of those who do not see that roughness is not a defect of the human condition, but what makes it work.

Reading the extract quoted above, I couldn't help thinking that, though Eagleton's remarks are clearly aimed at fundamentalists of the Islamic and Christian variety, the far left undoubtedly possesses a few unblinking fundamentalists of its own to whom his words might also perhaps apply!

For me, though, the most striking piece here is Éamonn McCann's 'Remembrance'. It deals with the arguments of the Kevin Myers tendency who argue that we should all wear poppies on Remembrance Day and 'celebrate' the memory of those tens of thousands of Irish who died in the First World War. Yes, McCann says, we should remember, but—and it's a big but:

We should have in our mind's eye in the season of Remembrance not the clean-cut youth of the gable murals rushing to death for God and Ulster; we should see him instead, from the Shankill or Falls, as he likely was.

And watch the white eyes writhing in his face,
His hanging face, like a devil's sick of sin;
If you could hear, at every jolt, the blood
Come gargling from the froth-corrupted lungs,
Obscene as cancer, bitter as the cud
Of vile, incurable sores on innocent tongues,
My friend, you would not tell with such high zest
To children ardent for some desperate glory,
The old lie: *Dulce et decorum est*
Pro patria mori.

The quote McCann uses to end his article is, of course, from Wilfred Owen's anti-war masterpiece 'Dulce et Decorum Est'. And it is perhaps a fitting way to draw this review towards a conclusion. All of these books are worth reading. But while the Faber and Faber anthology represents the anti-war poetry of the past, both *Irish Writers Against War* and *100 Poets Against The War* represent political literature in the here and now. There are, no doubt, one or two writers in them for whom the war was less about taking a stand than it was about jumping on the latest literary bandwagon. I recently heard someone quip that some Irish writers are so desperate for publication that they'd probably respond to an advert seeking submissions from writers of colour by immediately donning an Afro wig and singing 'Mammy'. But this is probably more or less as it has always been. All things considered, the editors have done an excellent job. Particularly when one considers how quickly these books had to be put together. Past struggles such as the Spanish Civil War and the movement against the Vietnam War have had their anthologies, and we now have ours.

Red Banner magazine, March 2004

Protest In Genoa

An Irishwoman's Diary
by Maureen Gallagher

As its title suggests this beautifully produced booklet, in which poet Maureen Gallagher tells from the inside the story of the huge anti-capitalist protest at the 2001 G8 summit, has ambitions to be both a personal memoir and a politically motivated pamphlet of the old variety. Its forty three glossy pages contain no less than twenty six photographs of the dramatic events in Genoa, during which one protestor, Carlo Giuliani, was shot dead by Italian police.

The fact that Gallagher is an accomplished poet of whom, I have no doubt, much more will be heard, gave me hope that this would amount to more than another political broadcast on behalf of the righteous and the dour. The result? Well, it's mixed. Gallagher is good at building drama, and succeeds admirably in giving the reader a sense of what it must have been like to face the tear gas and the riot police. In her description of the demonstration she shows us that, despite all the earnest faces, the anti-capitalist movement has a sense of humour too:

> "As we proceeded along the streets, women waved knickers and underpants from windows in defiance of Berlusconi's order that there was to be no underwear visible on clotheslines hanging from high rise flats."

Apparently, the Italian Prime Minister thought visiting dignitaries might be offended by the sight of Italian women's underwear. Elsewhere, though, *Protest In Genoa* falters rather: activists have conversations which are so banal that all one can do is hope they never actually happened:

"Keith told me that Jeffrey Archer... had just been sentenced to four years for corruption and contempt of court. 'It would be great to see some of our lot doing time for corruption', I remarked. 'Unfortunately, there wouldn't be enough room in your prisons for them!' Keith quipped."

And on page nine we are told:

"As it turned out, on Saturday night no one was in the least interested in Bob Dylan [who was in concert at a venue ten miles away] or his jaded performance: there were much more serious and real issues to be attended to."

For me this simply didn't ring true. No large group of people is ever that uniformly earnest: every demo has the guy who only came along in the hope that he might get laid. And, in my experience, he at least is always interested in talking about Bob Dylan.

Galway Advertiser, February 2004

Everything the Party did,
said and thought

Koba the Dread
by MARTIN AMIS

At the outset I should say that this is one of the most idiosyncratic books I've read in a long time. On one level it is simply a continuation of British novelist Martin Amis's attempt to work out his relationship with his father Kingsley, who died in 1991. Also a prominent literary figure in his time, Kingsley Amis is perhaps best known for his novel *Lucky Jim* (1954). Its hero Jim Dixon was a lower-middle-class radical whose aggressive anti-establishment, anti-pretension stance led some to associate Kingsley Amis with the group of 1950s British novelists and playwrights usually referred to as the Angry Young Men. And while Amis himself always resisted being associated with that particular grouping, he certainly shared much in common with them.

Like most of the Angries he started out as a left-wing radical (a member of the Communist Party from 1941 to 1956) and ended up somewhere to the right of Margaret Thatcher, whom he adored despite being disappointed that she never actually got around to shooting striking miners or sending the blacks back to Africa. Such minor frustrations aside, Kingsley Amis apparently ended his days relatively content with the general direction in which the world was headed. In his last book *Experience* (published in 2001) Martin Amis investigated his personal relationship with his father. Here he talks about his politics, taking issue, as one would perhaps expect, not with his later lurch to the right, but with his earlier support for Stalin.

On one side we have the rather pampered Martin, utterly

incapable of imagining for even five minutes a world fundamentally different from that which he sees around him. In many ways Martin Amis is the prototype post-cold war 'liberal'. Concerned, but not too concerned. The closest he's ever come to having a big idea is probably his belief in Tony Blair. Indeed, on page four Amis tells us that he began writing this book "a day or two" after spending the evening of 31 December 1999 at the Millennium Dome in London "along with Tony Blair and the Queen". He had apparently "recently read yards of books about the Soviet experiment".

On the other side we have his cranky father, Kingsley, talking about the loss he felt at letting go of his socialist beliefs: "The Ideal of the brotherhood of man, the building of the Just City, is one that cannot be discarded without lifelong feelings of disappointment and loss." Now, this is a feeling which every disappointed socialist must at some time have felt. Once the possibility of a New Society has raised itself seriously in your head, then there really is no going back. As a friend of mine puts it: "Whatever you do, you can never unlearn all you now know to be wrong with the world. You can never just get on with things in the same way again." When one thinks of it this way, it suddenly becomes rather less surprising that so many former revolutionaries end their days as monumental cranks, obsessively spitting poison at anything that even vaguely reminds them of what they themselves once were.

Now, if Martin Amis had restricted himself to writing about the obvious dichotomy between his father's politics and his own, then it could have made for an interesting, if not exactly earth-shattering little read. Instead, he insists on addressing what the book's jacket blurb describes as "the central lacuna of twentieth century thought: the indulgence of communism by intellectuals of the West". If Amis had at his disposal the intellectual equipment to deal properly with the issues involved, that would be one thing. But it so clearly isn't his area.

In places he ends up sounding like a loudmouthed student berating a Trotskyist newspaper-seller outside Trinity College. We are told that, among other things, "Trotsky was a murdering bastard and a fucking liar... He was a nun-killer—they all were". Surely, deep down, a writer of Amis's stature must realise that behind the failure of language explicit in such crude phraseology as "murdering bastard" and "fucking liar" lies a much more important failure of ideas? He can't quite prove his point, so he resorts instead to shouting abuse and stamping his feet.

Later we are told of Lenin's reaction to the famine which struck Czarist Russia in 1891:

> He [Lenin] 'had the courage', as a friend put it, to come out and say openly that famine would have numerous positive results... Famine, he explained, in destroying the outdated peasant economy, would... usher in socialism... Famine would also destroy faith not only in the tsar, but in God too.

Clearly this 'friend' of Lenin's was a nineteenth-century version of the sort of sad anorak who can sometimes still be found wandering around the fringes of the various far left organisations. You know the sort, the one with a slightly mad stare who thinks that what we really need to stir the masses into action is a sudden economic collapse followed immediately by a good long war. The key point here, though, is that the words belong not to Lenin, but to this unnamed 'friend'. If Amis wanted to convict Lenin of the crime of being indifferent to famine, then he really should have gone to the trouble of finding a quote from the man himself, rather than relying on such dodgy hearsay. It is true that Lenin believed that many of the famine relief schemes of the time were more about appearance than they were about reality: "In the regional capital of Samara only one intellectual, a twenty-two-year-old lawyer, refused to participate in the effort—and, indeed, publicly denounced it. This was Lenin." However, there's nothing very surprising about this. For example, there were many—and by no means all of them revolutionary socialists—who thought that the 1985 Live Aid concert was at least as much about ageing rock stars in general (and Bob Geldof in particular) salving their consciences and using the issue to get publicity for themselves, as it was about the Ethiopian famine. Surely what Lenin said back in 1891 amounted to nothing more than a nineteenth-century Russian version of the same thing?

Marxists are often accused, sometimes correctly so, of crude reductionist thinking. And yet here it is Amis who is desperate to simplistically collapse complex issues together. Marx is glibly dismissed as "a long dead German economist whose ideas [in the 1970s] were bringing biblical calamity to China, North Korea, Vietnam, Laos and Cambodia". Marxism = Stalinism. End of story. No mention of the fact that nowadays even many Wall Street economists regularly refer to the works of this "long dead German economist". To admit such an inconvenient fact would be to allow a shade of grey. And in this book Amis works only in black and white.

He makes no real attempt to differentiate between Stalinism and Trotskyism, preferring instead to pretend that they are one and the same thing. He asks his friend, the prominent British poet and onetime Trotskyist James Fenton: "How he... could align himself with a system that saw literature as a servant of the state; and, I thought, [you] must hate the language, the metallic cliches, the formulas and euphemisms". There is a vast reservoir of non-Stalinist Marxist literary criticism into which Amis could have dipped, if he was even slightly interested in getting a real answer to this question. But why bother with nuance, when caricature will do? Similarly, he tells another friend (and former Trotskyist) the essayist and critic Christopher Hitchens that "An admiration for... Trotsky is meaningless without an admiration for terror. [He] would not want your admiration without an admiration for terror. Do you admire terror?" It is as if the victims of the show trials of 1936 and 1938, such as Trotsky, Kamenev, Bukharin and Zinoviev, were as guilty as those who tortured and murdered them. Amis again and again accuses Marxists of being glib about human suffering, only to end up being very glib about it himself.

As far as I'm concerned, anyone who supported, or acted as an apologist for, regimes such as those in the Soviet Union, Eastern Europe, China and North Korea certainly has questions to answer. In case anyone out there needs reminding of just how rough it sometimes got in the so-called 'socialist' countries, here is a description of life in the Gulag:

> A group of prisoners at Kolyma were hungry enough to eat a horse that had been dead for more than a week (despite the stench and the infestation of flies and maggots). Scurvy makes the bones brittle; but then, 'Every prisoner welcomes a broken arm or leg.' Extra-large scurvy boils were 'particularly envied'. Admission to hospital was managed by quota. To get in with diarrhoea, you had to be evacuating (bloodily) every half hour. A man chopped off half his foot to get in there. And prisoners cultivated infections, feeding saliva, pus or kerosene to their wounds.

I personally would find it difficult to take very seriously anyone who ever so much as whispered an excuse for a regime such as this. Yes, we all make mistakes. But there are mistakes. And then again there are mistakes. However, there are, of course, also those on the left who never believed that the Soviet Union was any sort of paradise. The problem now is that we have all, to some extent, been painted with the same brush. To most people Marxism now either means failure or it means North Korea. And as soon as your average Joe and Josephine start thinking about North Korea, you can be sure it won't be long before they're also thinking how George W Bush isn't so bad after all.

Yes, *Koba the Dread* is in many ways an absurd book; so deficient that had its author not already been very famous, it would probably never have been accepted for publication by a reputable publisher. But in one sense that is neither here nor there. The real issue is what, if anything, the left can do to disentangle itself from Stalin's legacy? A few glib sentences here and there about North Korea being either 'state capitalist' or a 'deformed workers' state' are unlikely to be enough. The thing which above all else fatally undermined the revolutionary left in the twentieth century was the disastrous knack it developed—and I think some of the Trotskyist organisations are probably guilty here as well—of turning generation after generation of wide-eyed young activists into grim apologists for everything the Party did, said and thought. If the word 'socialism' is to have any relevance at all in the 21st century, then this is surely the issue which, above all else, must be addressed.

Red Banner magazine, December 2003

A critique of Red Lamp:

The journal of Realist, Socialist and Humanitarian poetry

It has often been said, that if only we (poets) spent less time pursuing the seemingly endless aesthetics versus politics argument, and more time actually writing poetry, then the world (or at least the part of it which appreciates poetry) would probably be a better place. After all, aren't we free to write whatever poetry we so choose? And it is certainly now possible (at least in the US and Britain) to find publishing outlets for almost any variety of poetry. Why don't you just get on with it?! So goes the frustrated cry of those who probably suspect that, deep down, we're the sort of people who like nothing better than to drone on all night about 'form versus content' until even the cat is desperately beseeching us, to please let her out in the rain! At least out there she won't have to listen to us whingeing on about L=A=N=G=U=A=G=E Poetry or Socialist Realism.

And I have to say that, despite the fact I really do think that there are important issues involved here; such as, for example, which poetic talents get nurtured, encouraged and promoted, and which suffer from neglect or are ignored; there have also been times when, like my metaphorical cat, I would have given anything to escape the sort of infantile carry on—the literary equivalent of a bad third division football match—which all too often passes for criticism/debate, between those who champion language for its own sake, and those who champion social/political content.

On one side we have the poetry 'aesthete', the guy who hangs around the poetry café all day long, a volume of L=A=N=G=U=A=G=E poetry in one hand, his *Portable Nietzsche* in the other, doing his bit for the avant-garde, with a little help from a tea cosy hat, probably knitted for him by his mother. Ask him what sort of poetry he likes and he'll tell you that, in his opinion, Clark Coolidge (who?!) is his generation's answer to Gertrude Stein. Hand him a copy of a meaningless poem in which 'Saddam Hussein's pyjamas' rhymes with 'llamas' and he will, I guarantee you, be very impressed. Tell him you wrote it and he'll probably tell you that, in his opinion, you're the next big thing, perhaps even, if you're lucky, your generation's answer to Clark Coolidge.

Meanwhile, on the other side of the table, sits the poetry-Bolshevik, the peak of his Russian cap at all times turned up to signify his utter contempt for all bourgeois authority. Look closely and you'll see, pinned to this selfsame cap, a small red star. Ask him where he got it and he'll proudly tell you that it originally belonged to his late uncle Stan, who was a member of the Communist Party and the Electrical Trades Union during the 1950s. Ask him what sort of poetry he likes and he'll probably mention Pablo Neruda, Vladimir Mayakovsky, Langston Hughes... Nothing wrong with that, you may say. But then show him a copy of a 'poem' you 'wrote' about fifteen years ago. Make it an angry/earnest broadside about the decline of an inner city area of, say, Liverpool or Glasgow under the Tories, and bring it to the following rapturous conclusion: "Thatcher is a cow. / Get her out now!" As he reads it, jabber on about how you submitted it to *The Times Literary Supplement*, *The London Review of Books*, *The New Yorker* etc, but that they all rejected it, preferring instead to publish the usual rubbish from the likes of Ashbery, Updike and Brodsky. As he hands you back your masterpiece, the poetry-Bolshevik will earnestly inform you that a bourgeois publication such as *The Times Literary Supplement* would never dream of publishing a political poem such as this. You'll smile wryly, say that you were naive to send it to them in the first place, and then he'll suggest that you should, perhaps, consider sending it to a magazine called *Red Lamp*. He has the address here somewhere...

Now, of course, I'm not suggesting that we should at all times be brutally honest, when it comes to other people's poetry. There are things like feelings to consider. And sometimes poets, particularly those from non-academic backgrounds, start off writing the sort of substandard political doggerel parodied above, but do, in time, improve to such an extent that they end up writing poems which have real artistic merit. So, we shouldn't come down on fledgling poets like a ton of bricks, while they're still trying to find their feet as best they can. But neither should we give false encouragement by helping substandard verse prematurely into print. The truth is that, in the long run, and sometimes even in the short run, this sort of help is no help at all, because once a mediocre poem is out in the public domain, even in a small magazine with a relatively modest print run, then it is fair game for hostile critics. And, as you well know, there is absolutely no shortage of them.

A magazine such as *Red Lamp* could become an important meeting place for poets who are outside the political mainstream, a place where the issues, which we constantly come up against, such as, for example, the disastrous legacy of Stalinist Socialist Realism, could be properly dealt with. It could also provide a forum for the development of a thoughtful critique of the rest of the poetry world. Why not review the latest collections by big name poets such as, say, Simon Armitage, Carol Ann Duffy or Paul Durcan? Surely we must have something to say about all of them. There is so much more that we could be doing.

But as things stand, *Red Lamp* is, I think, in some danger of becoming a magazine content to preach to a dwindling band of converts. The fact is that, worldwide, there probably aren't enough talented politically conscious poets to fill your pages with quality work issue after issue. (And quality is definitely what we should all be aiming at.) So, in one sense, it's hardly surprising, that there are several poems in issue 9, which fall far short of what's required. Meryl Brown Tobin's *Poem of Witness* is one example:

After days of massacre,
Indonesia allows
U.N. in.
Australia leads.
'Vested interests
in oil,' cry protestors.
Multi-millionaire chides:
'Australia's going in solely
on humanitarian grounds—
She should think about
economic and trade concerns.'
What price humanity?

As poetry this sort of thing is an unmitigated disaster. The language is not in the slightest bit fresh or inventive. And the opinions expressed are nothing that a Blair/Clinton pseudo-liberal couldn't at least pretend to agree with. Even in terms of content, it falls absolutely flat. And Steven Katsineris's *For Unity and Equality* is no better. It starts off weakly enough,

> If you're Anglo-Australian then you don't know how it feels
> to be born ethnic in Australia.
> To be verbally abused or worse,
> made to feel you're off the last boat...

But it was the last few lines that really made me cringe,

> If you're Anglo-Australian you can't really know how it feels,
> that's not your fault, but you can try to listen, learn and understand.
> And let Aboriginal and Ethnic Australians know
> they don't stand alone, that many Anglo-Australians
> stand alongside them too, standing up for unity and equality.

Well meaning it may be, but good poetry it most definitely is not. Reading a poem like this is, for me, about as aesthetically pleasing as bathing in cold porridge. It is offensive on two levels. Firstly, as someone who has, on occasion, spent days (if not weeks) struggling to find exactly the right words to make a poem as complete as I possibly can, I find the bland, lazy language astonishing. And secondly, I know perfectly well that this is exactly the sort of poem which hostile reviewers will use to beat everyone who contributes to *Red Lamp* over the head with. "This is what happens", they will tell us, "when you try to mix poetry and politics..." And we can hardly blame them. If you offer the opposing team an open goal, then you forfeit the right to complain, when they stick the ball in the back of the net.

There were, of course, also a number of good poems in issue 9, such as Julie Ashpool's *Sister* and Vincent Berquez's *Hunter of Work?*, for example. And I particularly liked Susan Stanford's *Poor Man*:

> Dismissed, shrinking into himself, he inhales
> the poisons of two packs a day. What's the point
> now? He's out of the picture. Vision's become
> another management buzzword. Life's gritty,
> takes longer. He walks or travels by bus,
> does his washing by hand. Food's just short enough
> for thought to be called for. He mashes sardines.
> Puts a match to the gas. Feels the cold at the tip
> of his nose. A moment of toast in the mouth.

But as *Red Lamp* goes on, poems of the inferior variety increasingly seem to predominate. And it was that fact which spurred me to write this piece. The criticisms I make are made only in the hope of stirring up a constructive debate from which a stronger magazine might perhaps emerge...

The Journal, Spring 2002

Palaces of memory,
rooms full of light

In The Blue House
by MEAGHAN DELAHUNT

Meaghan Delahunt's debut novel—a fictionalised version of Leon
Trotsky's last years in Mexico and, in particular, his relationship
with the artist Frida Kahlo—bucks a number of the trends which
have lately come to dominate the rather precious world of
contemporary English language fiction. Given the typically oh so
self-obsessed novels about getting divorced in Hampstead (à la
Martin Amis) or going to find yourself in Spain (à la Colm Tóibín)
which currently dominate the bookshelves in Eason's and
Waterstones, it was refreshing indeed to find a novel in which
history, far from being over, is writ large; and to encounter
characters who, for better or for worse, actually mattered in the
grand scheme of things. However, perhaps the way this novel
differs from most of its contemporaries is best illustrated by the fact
that I actually managed to read it from beginning to end—all 304
pages—without once being tempted to see what was on the
television. Episode after episode of *Home and Away* and *The Bold
and the Beautiful* drifted into oblivion as it grabbed and held my
attention.

Delahunt successfully weaves the messy details of Trotsky's
personal life (such as the affair with Kahlo and its aftermath) and
the tumultuous events of his political life into an impressively
seamless whole. To do this she uses an occasionally bewildering
variety of narrators, everyone from Trotsky and Kahlo themselves
to Stalin, Beria, the poet Mayakovsky and Ramon Mercader, the
man who eventually wielded that ice-pick. She also skips around
considerably in time. For example, the story 'starts' shortly after

Frida Kahlo's death in July 1954 with Señora Rosita Moreno reminiscing about Kahlo's life in the Blue House of the title. On page 175, though, we're suddenly back in 1898 and the young Trotsky is pacing around his first ever prison cell in Odessa. Changing narrator with each chapter, Delahunt's version of the story moves relentlessly back and forth through time before ending back where it began with Frida Kahlo's death in 1954. A structure which in the hands of a less accomplished writer could have made the novel confusing and episodic actually works very well.

The chapters are short and punchy, and almost entirely devoid of self-indulgent first novel rambling. The book apparently evolved from a short story of Delahunt's, 'In the Blue House at Coyoacan', which was published in the Australian literary magazine *Heat* back in 1998. And one gets the impression that it has been through several drafts. Facing into a story like this must have been an absolutely daunting task for a first-time novelist such as Delahunt. To begin with, the fact that it is based on the lives of prominent historical figures, who were alive as recently as the middle of the last century, means that you need more than dramatic tension to keep the reader interested. Hardly anyone will read on simply to find out 'what happened in the end', because the vast majority of Delahunt's potential readers will already have known at least the basics of the 'Trotsky story' long before they picked up her book. Of course, one definite advantage *In The Blue House* has from the outset is that, quite unlike the typical Hampstead divorcee, its characters are all such interesting people.

It is, above all else, a book about Trotsky's personal reaction to the devastating political defeats he suffered during the last decade and a half of his life. As Delahunt tells it, his affair with Frida Kahlo was something of an attempt to recapture his former glory at a time when, deep down, he knew perfectly well that his days were numbered:

> He had seen himself new, had felt as if all the accumulations of his past had been rolled back in the body of a person much younger than himself who knew only the grandeur of him and none of its fading.
>
> For Natalia [his wife] knew the lustre. She knew, also, the efforts to maintain it, to polish. The effort, sometimes, to keep going.
>
> The younger woman saw none of this, and this cheered

him. Made him forget how much effort it took to rise again in the morning, preparing for battle, wondering if that day would be his last and, if that were the case, how best to live it.

How different this Trotsky is from the caricature 'Strelnikov' in *Doctor Zhivago* with his deadpan declaration about the personal life now being "dead in Russia". Much has been made of the way Trotsky supposedly shrugged off even the most devastating political setbacks. And no doubt he had an amazing capacity for picking himself up and starting from scratch again. However, I have to say that I think Delahunt does us a service by making her Trotsky rather more completely human than the one we are used to. Shortly before his death in August 1940 she has him suffering from insomnia and wondering if he had "like Marx, neglected those closest to him? Made intolerable demands upon them?... Maybe he had no talent for love or intimacy." Some will undoubtedly read these thoughts as belonging more to Delahunt than to Trotsky, and as such will see them as the self-justification of someone who simply hadn't the stomach for the long, hard haul of revolutionary politics. However, this would, I think, be a crude reading to say the least. After all, who among those of us who've had any sort of serious involvement in revolutionary politics has not, on occasion, paused to consider the toll that involvement has taken on their personal life?

My favourite passage, though, is on page 253 in a chapter narrated by Trotsky's wife Natalia:

> Of course, later, when personal tragedy consumed us, when we lost everyone [including all of their children]... He would stand at the window and look up at the moon. He would pack the dead away inside himself. So many spaces for the dead inside. We spoke often of our palaces of memory. In these rooms our children still played. Friends still embraced; we clinked glasses in rooms full of light. But some rooms, after we had endured too much, could never be opened.

Though this is clearly a description of a deeply personal tragedy, it could also be read as a sustained metaphor for the complete crushing of revolutionary optimism in any time or place. And, while it would certainly be ludicrous to make any direct comparison between the relatively small sacrifices activists today sometimes make and the gothic tragedy which engulfed Trotsky, there are, I think, many of us who know something about what it's like to have long-lost comrades with whom we still occasionally clink glasses in imaginary "rooms full of light". As a former Trotskyist activist herself, Delahunt clearly knows what she's talking about here. However, far from being some dry political tract, *In The Blue House* is, on the contrary, a very accomplished work of art indeed. By avoiding hero worship and, instead, painting this picture of a decidedly fallible Trotsky grappling with the consequences of a catastrophic political defeat, Delahunt succeeds in making him someone the contemporary reader can really believe in.

Red Banner magazine, March 2002

Borges, Balzac and the Ghost of Christmas Yet To Come

Unacknowledged Legislation: Writers in the public sphere
by CHRISTOPHER HITCHENS

To say that the relationship between literary criticism and Marxist politics has been fraught with difficulties is something of an understatement. More often than not the nuanced, dialectical approach used by the likes of Marx and Trotsky to unravel the world of literature in all its many-sided complexity has been (and for the most part still is) elbowed aside in favour of a crude reductionism which has its origins in the Stalinist crackdown on literature and art in the late 1920s. Even today, those who review books (or films) for left-wing publications tend to operate on the basis that if a book is 'objectively speaking' on the right side of the class struggle then this, in and of itself, must mean that the book in question is a 'good book' deserving a positive review. And the reverse is also held to be true: T S Eliot's poetry couldn't possibly be a patch on, say, Jimmy McGovern's *Dockers* because, after all, T S Eliot was a reactionary. In the minds of some, any comrade who takes a few hours out from the class struggle to read *The Wasteland or The Love Song of J Alfred Prufrock* is probably in serious danger of ending up on the Fine Gael front bench, or as Primate of the Church of Ireland, or some such grotesque bourgeois deviation.

Roddy Doyle is judged to be more 'politically relevant' than, say, John Updike or Julian Barnes, merely because he writes about 'ordinary working class people', whereas they for the most part don't. And indeed perhaps he is more relevant, at least in the sense that his subject matter means that socialists will probably have more to say about him than they will about most contemporary novelists. However, taken too far, this sort of approach to literature and art could, at least in theory, reduce us to the absurdity of saying that Brendan Grace is somehow a better comedian than Woody Allen merely because his subject matter is more 'working-class'; or, perhaps a little more plausibly, that Rage Against The Machine are definitely better than Elgar was, because they sing "fuck the police" whereas he did nothing of the sort. Marx and Engels may have thought that, in literary terms, one reactionary Balzac, writing as he did predominantly about the French middle and upper classes, was preferable to a hundred socialist Zolas, writing about 'the workers', but such dialectical niceties tend unfortunately to be lost on most of their followers.

In this context, Christopher Hitchens' *Unacknowledged Legislation: Writers in the public sphere* is required reading for anyone even remotely interested in the relationship between literature and politics. And how ironic it is that this example of a dialectical (one might say almost Marxist) approach to literature should be provided by Hitchens: a 'left' liberal Vanity Fair columnist, who since September 11 has apparently lost the run of himself and become (along with silly old Paul McCartney) just another raving imperialist warmonger. It is, as Margaret Thatcher once famously remarked, a funny old world indeed.

The book is a collection of thirty five reviews and essays, which originally appeared in publications such as T*he New York Review of Books*, the *New Left Review* and the *Times Literary Supplement*. In the foreword Hitchens tells us about the influence Wilfred Owen's devastatingly powerful anti-war poem 'Dulce Et Decorum Est' had on him as a young man:

I shall never be able to forget the way in which these verses utterly turned over all the furniture in my mind; inverting every conception of order and patriotism and tradition on which I had been brought up. I hadn't yet encountered, or even heard of the novels of Barbusse and Remarque, or the paintings of Otto Dix, or the great essays and polemics of the Zimmerwald and Kienthal conferences; the appeals to civilisation written by Rosa Luxemburg in her *Junius* incarnation. (Revisionism has succeeded in overturning many of the icons of Western Marxism; this tide however still halts when it confronts the nobility of Luxemburg and Jean Jaures and other less celebrated heroes of 1914—such as the Serbian Dimitri Tucovic.) I came to all these discoveries, and later ones such as the magnificent *Regeneration* trilogy composed by Pat Barker, through a door that had been forced open for me by Owen's 'Dulce Et Decorum Est'.

All the more ironic, then, that in the aftermath of September 11 Hitchens has apparently turned his back on the tradition of Zimmerwald and Rosa Luxemburg, preferring instead to accuse opponents of the War on Terrorism of being 'soft on fascism' in an article in *The Spectator*: a magazine which has in its time given refuge to every rightward moving crank from Kingsley Amis to Woodrow Wyatt.

A little further on in the foreword Hitchens points out that:

> Many of the writers discussed here have no 'agenda' of any sort, or are conservatives whose insight and integrity I have found indispensable. I remember for example sitting with Jorge Luis Borges in Buenos Aires as he employed an almost Evelyn Waugh-like argument in excusing the military dictatorship that then held power in his country. But I had a feeling that he couldn't keep up this pose, and not many years later he wrote a satirical poem ridiculing the Falklands/Malvinas adventure while also making statements against the junta's cruelty in the matter of the *desaparecidos*. It wasn't just another author signing a letter about 'human rights'; it was the ironic mind refusing the dictates of the literal one.

This sort of talk will probably sound fairly alien to most left-wing activists, brought up as most of us have been on a diet of 'Ken Loach good, *Brideshead Revisited* bad'. And yet it is far closer to Marx's actual approach to literature—Borges perhaps being a kind of latter-day Argentinian Balzac—than anything you're likely to read in an issue of a far left paper. A little more commonplace is Hitchens' observation that:

> In the case of the United States, we await a writer who can summon every nerve to cleanse the country of the filthy stain of the death penalty... there is as yet no Blake or Camus or Koestler to synthesise justice and reason with outrage; to compose the poem or novel—as did Herman Melville with flogging in his *White-Jacket*—*that will constitute the needful* moral legislation.

Of course the well-meaning sentiments are undoubtedly already there, indeed are probably ten-a-penny at every open-mike poetry night from Greenwich Village to San Francisco, but the trick is to combine the political and the aesthetic: to accomplish the usually impossible task of making a statement which as well as being 'true' is memorable to the point of being in some sense beautiful.

The writers with whom Hitchens engages here range from the predictable—George Orwell, Raymond Williams, Gore Vidal, Salman Rushdie and Oscar Wilde—to those such as F Scott Fitzgerald and Roald Dahl whose work might superficially seem to be almost entirely devoid of political content. 'Rebel in Evening Clothes' is the title of a lovely essay on Dorothy Parker who, as a daughter of the massively wealthy Rothschild family and fashion writer for *Vogue*, was perhaps an unlikely radical. And yet her 1919 poem, originally titled 'Hate Song', is something which, with the possible exception of a slightly disparaging reference to milkmen, even the most hardened Socialist Realist would surely have to appreciate:

> ...the Boss;
> He made us what we are to-day—
> I hope he's satisfied.
> He has some bizarre ideas
> About his employees getting to work
> At nine o'clock in the morning—
> As if they were a lot of milkmen.
> He has never been known to see you
> When you arrive at 8.45,
> But try to come in at a quarter past ten
> And he will always go up in the elevator with you.
> He goes to Paris on the slightest provocation
> And nobody knows why he has to stay there so long.

There are also some hilarious demolition jobs: on the horribly glib Tom Wolfe (essayist and author of the novel *Bonfire of the Vanities*); on Tom Clancy (author of *The Hunt for Red October* etc, etc) who Hitchens aptly describes as "the junk supplier of surrogate testosterone"; and, best of all, on the prominent American critic Norman Podhoretz, of whom he says: "But as the years passed... Podhoretz began to fawn more openly on Richard Nixon and the Israeli general staff as if rehearsing for the engulfing, mandible-straining blow job he would later bestow on Ronald Reagan." Of course, in the light of his own post-September 11 descent into pro-imperialist jingoism, it is entirely possible that, for Hitchens himself, that particular sentence might yet turn out to be the Ghost of Christmas Yet To Come.

However, the best essay in the entire book is his examination of the life and poetry of Philip Larkin. Ever since the publication of his *Selected Letters* in 1992 showed that he was, to put it mildly, a reactionary and a racist, critical responses to Larkin have tended to polarise into two distinct camps. On the left are those who claim that the fact that Larkin enclosed the following charming little ditty in a letter to a friend clearly exposes him as the disgusting reactionary they always suspected him of being:

Prison for the strikers
Bring back the cat
Kick out the niggers
How about that?

And for Larkin's critics this is where the case for the prosecution usually rests. Meanwhile his apologists such as the critic John Bailey have claimed that Larkin was simply "more free of cant—political, social or literary—than any of his peers". Britain's current Poet Laureate Andrew Motion has even gone so far as to say "that Larkin's work had the capacity to create a recognisable and democratic vision of contemporary society". Hitchens cuts through both hypocrisy and hyperbole with great skill, providing us with pretty damning evidence that, far from being just another Tory Little Englander, Larkin was in fact a "frustrated fascist", who after 1945 was forced by the new political realities to hide his real political beliefs. And yet at the same time Hitchens still manages to separate the poems themselves from the political views of the poet:

unless we lose all interest in contradiction—we are fortunate in being able to say that Larkin's politics are buried well beneath, and somewhere apart from, his poems. The place he occupies in popular affection—which he had won for himself long before the publication of his fouler private thoughts—is the place that he earned, paradoxically, by attention to ordinariness, to quotidian suffering and to demotic humour. Decaying communities, old people's homes, housing estates, clinics... he mapped these much better than most social democrats, and he found words for experience.

Unacknowledged Legislation is a truly excellent book: a must for anyone who has ever complained about one of those left-press reviews in which the reviewer typically uses the last sentence to earnestly inform us that the 'fundamental flaw' in this or that book or film is that nowhere does it provide the working class with an answer to the problems they face under capitalism. The recent political statements of its author, Christopher Hitchens, are of course disappointing in the extreme; but they are also perhaps just a contemporary example of the relationship between literature and politics in all its complexity.

Red Banner magazine, December 2001

Famine, Fundamentalism
and Suicide Bombers

Since September 11th, the sympathy we all feel for those who lost loved ones in the attack on the World Trade Center has been used to try and create an atmosphere in which those of us who oppose the U.S. led military intervention in Afghanistan will feel intimidated, and remain silent. The first argument typically used against us is to say that we are simply displaying an entirely predictable knee-jerk anti-Americanism. After all, aren't we the people who never have a good word to say about the United States, whatever it does anywhere in the world?

The clever thing about this argument is that it does, of course, have some truth in it. Albeit only a grain. Yes, I have to agree, I honestly can't remember the last time I had a good word to say about the role the U.S. government has played and does play around the world. But this is not because of some sort of irrational 'anti-Americanism' on my part, as the use of the term "knee-jerk" implies. It is, quite simply, because, be it Indonesia, Chile or Saudi Arabia (the list is almost endless but they'll do to be going on with) when it comes to U.S. foreign policy, there really are very few good words to be said.

However, I should say at this point, that in no sense do I hold the ordinary Americans I know personally in any way responsible for 'their' government's policies. As an Irish person I would be horrified if someone saw Charlie McGreevy or Mary Harney as in any sense 'representing' me. So, it would be ludicrous for me to blame, say, my friend Randolph from Minneapolis for what George W. Bush is currently doing in Afghanistan.

George W. Bush talks endlessly about a war in defence of "freedom and democracy". And yet this year alone, the U.S. government will give €3 billion worth of military aid to the Saudi

Arabian government: a brutal dictatorship which implements most of the same repressive Sharia Islamic laws as the Taliban does. In Saudi Arabia there is no freedom, no democracy. And the military aid the U.S. gives its government is designed to make sure that it stays that way. Of course the American people are never actually asked if they want their tax dollars spent on propping up this oil-rich 'friendly' dictatorship. And the policy was exactly the same under Clinton, and would have continued had Gore won the election. When they all offer you the same rotten policy, democracy really does become something of a meaningless abstraction.

Another accusation I've heard levelled at us, is that our reaction has been 'cold and emotionless'. Now, while there may have been one or two rather sad individuals who have simply used this as yet another opportunity to parrot the same dead old slogans—aren't there always?—they are definitely not the majority. Personally, all I can say is that since I flew back from a brief holiday in the U.K. on the evening of September 10th, almost everything I have done has in some way been impacted by what took place the following day. It has in no sense been business as usual.

Which is more than can be said for Jo Moore, one of Tony Blair's spin-doctors. At 2.55pm on Tuesday, September 11th, less than an hour after the first plane crashed into the World Trade Center, Moore sent an email to Blair's Transport Minister Stephen Byers telling him: *"After what's just happened today. This must be an ideal time to get rid of any 'bad news' announcements you might want to bury."* To date, Blair has steadfastly refused to fire her. Apparently Tony is quite turned on by her ideas about the privatising the London Underground.

Tony Blair has again and again described this war as being, above all else, a war for 'justice'. This cleverly taps into the understandable feeling most people have that, after more than 5,000 deaths, someone must surely be brought to book. To ascertain Tony Blair's real attitude to justice we need to cast our minds back to another, now almost forgotten, September massacre.

September 11th, 1973: the day the democratically elected government of Salvador Allende was overthrown in a military coup in Chile, aided and abetted by the C.I.A. In the aftermath of the coup several thousand people were herded into the national stadium in Santiago, where they were tortured or killed.

Last year the Spanish government asked the British to extradite General Pinochet, leader of that coup, to stand trial in Spain for his part in the murder of Spanish citizens in Chile. But rather than send Pinochet to face justice, Tony Blair's government let him go free on the grounds that he was supposedly 'unfit to stand trial'. Now, when you let General Pinochet go free you must surely forfeit the right to talk about justice, even for Osama Bin Laden. I'm sorry Tony, but you really can't have it both ways.

The war aims of the ongoing attack on Afghanistan are now becoming clear. A pro-Western coalition government will be installed in Kabul. This government will include the Northern Alliance, the eighty six year old former King and possibly, even, some 'moderate' elements of the Taliban (whatever the word 'moderate' is supposed to mean in this context). Then, when Bush and Blair have had their fun, the people of Afghanistan will be left to rot once again. The entire Middle East has been turned into a nightmare zone by decades of such self-serving western intervention. In this context, the attack on Afghanistan simply represents more of the same. And the result will similarly be more of the same. More famine, more fundamentalism, and, of course, more suicide bombers. Do you really want to sign up for all that?

Muc Mhór Dhubh (edited by Rab Fulton) November 2001

Whatever happened to
the end of history?

When an important meeting of the World Trade Organisation in Seattle was seriously disrupted by a couple of hundred thousand anti-capitalist demonstrators in December 1999, it came as a big surprise to almost everyone. But as the year 2000 unfolded, and similar demonstrations turned meetings of the International Monetary Fund, the World Bank and the European Union into platforms for the 'anti-capitalists', it became perfectly clear that Seattle was anything but a flash in the pan. Be it Prague, Melbourne or Washington DC, wherever the decision-makers of the ruling global elite went, the 'anti-capitalists' followed them. And this wasn't how the script was supposed to go at all. Politics of this sort was supposed to be a thing of the past.

The 'anti-capitalism' born in Seattle represents a radical departure from the sort of polite, middle class environmentalism we had grown used to during the apathetic 1990s. Indeed one of the most significant things about the Seattle demonstration was that it attracted support not only from environmentalists (and large groups of anarchists) but also from both Mexican workers and American trade unions (such as the Teamsters) protesting against the detrimental effects of Bill Clinton's great free-market 'achievement', the North American Free Trade Agreement (NAFTA).

While this movement is still very much in its infancy, it represents a significant step forward if we place it in the context of the political malaise of the past twenty years or so. The 1980s and early 90s were years of almost unrivalled capitalist triumphalism. Organised labour was everywhere on the retreat as the labour market was 'deregulated'. Reagan broke the air-traffic controllers' strike of 1981 and, in the process, destroyed their union PATCO, while his ideological twin Thatcher made an example of the miners during their year long strike in 1984/85. And then came the collapse of 'Communism'. This gave capitalism a powerful ideological weapon which its propagandists used to paint all versions of Marxism and socialism as offshoots of the same failed, totalitarian system. It was all one way traffic. Capitalism had never had it so easy.

During the years that followed, apathy towards politics grew until, by the late 90s, it was overwhelming. Many left-wing activists, myself included, simply gave up the struggle and immersed themselves in private life or the arts or whatever took our fancy. It was less a case of 'selling out' than of having grown rather tired. Most of us stuck to the fundamental belief that socialism still represented a far saner, more rational way of organising things than chaotic, profit-driven capitalism ever could but, in the hostile climate of the 1990s, we could see no meaningful way of advancing this cause. And all around us were the false prophets of the New World Order. In his book *The Last Man and The End of History* (1990), American academic Francis Fukuyama argued that history was now "over" and that "liberal capitalism" had "triumphed". Wall Street would rule the world for a thousand years. For us this amounted to something more awful than even our worst nightmare. All we could do was seethe, while EuroDisney tried to buy Lenin's body. Of course, in the years 1991-99, people did still protest, go on strike etc. But it was as if the socialist movement, the labour movement had been castrated. After all, if everyone accepts the 'free' market, then the scope for real political change is very limited indeed.

Some of my more politically 'sensible' friends will undoubtedly protest that the picture I am painting here is just a little too black. Weren't the 1990s a time of some, albeit modest, political progress, with a Labour government in Britain, and a 'liberal' Democrat in the White House? But if we look beyond the slick phrases of the spin-doctors and examine the reality we find that, on every single important issue, Blair and Clinton continued the policies of their Republican and Tory predecessors. On welfare, Clinton continued, indeed accelerated, the cutbacks started by Reagan and George Bush Senior. On the death penalty, Clinton was the first Democrat in a long while to so enthusiastically support it, even taking time out from campaigning in New Hampshire in 1992 to go back to Arkansas and sign a death warrant for a mentally retarded black man, Rickey Ray Rector. Clinton's one liberal promise—on health care—very quickly came to nothing. Tony Blair is, if anything, a little further to the right than 'Slick Willy'. One of his government's first acts was to cut social security payments to single mothers. Since then his 'Labour' government has taken the 'radical' step of ending free third level education, something even Thatcher never dared to do. I could go on, but you get the picture.

Of course, both of these gentlemen have been strong advocates of 'economic globalisation'. However the 'globalisation' they have supported is 'global' only as long as that serves the interests of the economic elite. Microsoft et al can move their operations with impunity to wherever labour is most 'competitively priced'. If American workers demand higher wages, they can always move, for example, to Ireland, and if the Irish start getting a bit uppity, there's always Eastern Europe. Under NAFTA, American companies have unrestricted access to a large supply of cheap labour in Mexico, and yet the US/Mexican border remains one of the most patrolled borders in the world. Illegal immigrants are hunted down. And, a little closer to home, a crooked Irish politician such as Liam Lawlor can invest his dodgy money in Czech banks, but an ordinary Czech person cannot, as things currently stand, come and live in Ireland. Western companies make easy money in Eastern Europe but the EU's 'Fortress Europe' anti-immigration policy means that immigrants coming in the opposite direction will, most likely, be stopped by the police and held in detention centres. These are the stark realities of capitalist 'globalisation'. But since Seattle these policies are, at long last, facing some serious opposition.

The Economist magazine recently commented:

> Many business people dismiss these [anti-capitalist] protests as nothing more than a distraction. They argue that globalisation is being driven by technology and that there is nothing that anybody, including Molotov-cocktail throwing demonstrators, can do to put the genie back in the bottle. This is profoundly wrong... Activists have already seized the initiative on global trade... Many companies [have been] lulled into a false sense of security by years of pro-market reforms...

This is not to say that capitalism is about to be overthrown by a rag-tag movement whose calling card to date has been to try and burn down at least one branch of McDonald's in every city where leaders of the World Bank, the EU or the IMF happen to be meeting. If only it were that simple. But those who engage in such naive forms of 'direct action' are at least groping in the right direction. And while reserving the right to offer constructive criticism, we should at the same time recognise the fact that this movement has succeeded in raising the banner of anti-capitalism for all to see once again, just when many on the left had given up hope altogether.

It has also put its finger firmly on the fundamental reality that, since capitalism has gone global, the opposition to it should similarly be organised across national boundaries. The official labour and trade union movement has been paying lip-service to this idea for decades now, but the anti-capitalists have found new imaginative ways of actually putting it into practice, and in the space of a few months, have succeeded in putting more pressure on organisations such as the IMF than a hundred years of whiny speeches by the likes of Bono ever possibly could.

During the 1990s many on the left were hypnotised into a state of almost unrelieved gloom by the seemingly endless mantra about the End of History. But when such an august bourgeois publication as The Economist is prepared to recognise the reality that the ladies and gentlemen who sit in the boardrooms of the global corporations can no longer expect to have everything their own way as easily as they did in the 80s and 90s, it must surely be time even the left's most ardent pessimists allowed something approaching a smile to flicker across their faces.

Red Banner magazine, September 2001

First publications from Tribes are a fascinating mix

The Heron by Lesley Sargent (33pp 2.99pb), *Man of Allah* by Barkat Ali Masood (49pp 2.99pb) and *Glorious Purple* by Frances Joyce (45pp 2.99pb) were all published recently by Tribes. At the outset, it should be said, that Tribes—the result of an innovative collaboration between English students at NUIG and local poet/editor Rab Fulton—is a very welcome addition to the local publishing scene. And it is good to see that they have used this, their first outing, as an opportunity to bring us these three diverse new voices, when they could so easily have played it much safer.

Lesley Sargent's *The Heron* is a long short story, which uses the idea of reincarnation to explore our relationships, and particularly, the misunderstandings which constantly arise between us. Given this theme, it is perhaps not surprising that she uses several different voices, rather than an omniscient narrator, to tell her tale. Central is the relationship between David and his girlfriend. He wants to move the relationship onto another level, while she is thinking that, if only she could get rid of him, she could revert to her "single, uncomplicated life". David tells her he loves her after taking her hand "over the romance-laden table" in a restaurant. But glancing around at the other couples "on their own little islands" she asks him rather coldly "what he means by that?" Understandably frustrated, David loses it and ends up storming out. Outside he is mowed down by a passing drunk driver, only to be reincarnated as a fish. However, his troubles are only beginning. He's swimming around in the river one day, when he sees her passing by and notices that she's pregnant. At all costs he has to be near her. So he commits suicide by feeding himself to a heron, and this time comes back as a bluebottle. On one level this is something of a demotion. But at least it means that he can be near her and his child. Not that they'll know it's him of course. Such is life, Sargent seems to be saying. The only real reservation I have arose here. On page 13 David says: "I'm fortunate to know that the taking of one's own life results in us joining a lower karmic order." Now, I've heard karma (a kind of metaphysical what-goes-around-comes-around) used to explain away everything from autism to the Holocaust. It is a concept which tends to lead people towards some very questionable ideas indeed. So, *The Heron* is perhaps best read as an allegory for the fraught situations life sometimes forces us into, rather than as a tale to be taken too literally. That said, Lesley Sargent is clearly a writer to watch out for. Her prose manages to be poetic without being overwritten. And she moves the story relentlessly onwards, with great skill, towards its tragicomic conclusion.

Barkat Ali Masood's *Man of Allah* is a more straightforward narrative. The story of an Irish born man of Pakistani origin, caught between two cultures, *Man of Allah* is an example of the sort of transcultural literature of which we are likely to see much more. All too often literary attempts at multiculturalism amount to nothing more than a room full of white liberals politely telling each other that racism is bad, while at the same time desperately trying to avoid saying anything which might offend the minister for arts. But Barkat Ali Masood is light years away from all that. He takes us on a roller-coaster journey, all the way from, "Wonderfully smelly dusty dry hotty Lahore! A modern city with modern architecture and modern tarmac roads and modern brown people covered by the blanket of yellowy dust and browny dirt" to a nightclub in Galway, where the main character Salman is going about his business in the lavatory, when he notices "a pair of legs in loafers facing two legs in tights" in the cubicle next door. Forced to listen as the couple next-door's passion reaches its climax, Salman is even more downcast when he realises that the "lucky bastard" in question is one of those "hated rugby jocks". Now, I don't visit such establishments as regularly as I used to. But, nevertheless, something about this definitely rings true. His sad nightclub exploits aside, Salman seems destined to feel like a foreigner wherever he goes. An outsider in Ireland, he is, if anything, even less at home in Pakistan. Masood deals with all this in a way that is not at all heavy handed, and displays a considerable talent for understated comedy.

Glorious Purple by Frances Joyce is a collection of poetry. In poems such as 'The Stopper', 'A Mother-In-Law's Tongue' and

'The English Class' Frances Joyce shows that, with her light ironic touch, she might yet give the likes of Wendy Cope and Rita Ann Higgins a run for their money. 'The English Class' was my favourite. "Eliot, Graves, Pinter, Shaw, / Conrad, Shakespeare, Lawrence, Waugh / Maybe too many male hormones? / There were no women writer's on the syllabus. / White-winged phalluses: / I imagined them flying / Around the room like angels, / Or jumping from desk to desk / like sausages on springs." Elsewhere she shows that she can be lyrical as well. I particularly liked the first stanza of '31.12.2000'. "The souls of the Claddagh / Gathered as the church-bells failed to ring. / Seashells echoed their silent voice / From Boston to Birmingham / And the waves lapped gently against the pier / While two late-night gulls played a game of tag, / Chasing trade winds, / Oblivious to the solemnity of the moment." However, as it goes on, this poem seems to run out steam. And by the time you reach the lines "A Fairytale of New York / Drifted from a Hotel" in the fifth stanza, the imagery, initially so fresh, has become rather stale. It has to be said that several of the poems here are in need of surgery. The opening stanza of the title poem is a case in point, "I dreamed a dream / In glorious purple / Of a place / Where love flowed / From the skies / Like Galway rain." It might work as greeting card verse, but as poetry it simply doesn't wash. And in 'Someone Will Die' with lines such as "The Roman / And the Gael / Together / Intoning / Shanti. Shanti, Shanti.", she seems to mistake the statement of good intentions for good literature. However, despite this occasionally shaky start, there is enough promise here to make Frances Joyce a name to look out for in the future.

Galway Advertiser, August 16th, 2001

Unmasking the real enemy

Asylum-seekers and other non-white economic migrants first began arriving here in significant numbers during the late 1990s. The numbers involved are still relatively small—not much more than 10,000 expected this year—but, nevertheless, the sight of Romanian women selling the *Big Issues* and black men driving second hand cars have become increasingly familiar features of the urban Irish landscape. The reasons for the sudden appearance in Ireland of people from Eastern Europe and Africa are twofold.

Firstly, there has been a general increase in the numbers of immigrants entering the EU, legally and otherwise. And it's not hard to see why. Several African countries, such as Sierra Leone, Liberia and the Congo Republic, have been torn apart by a series of particularly disastrous civil wars. The oil-company-friendly military dictatorship in Nigeria—Africa's second richest country after South Africa—has been cracking down on even the mildest forms of dissent. And post-Stalinist Eastern Europe has faced economic collapse and ethnic strife which, in the case of the former Yugoslavia, reached genocidal proportions. Prague and Budapest may be the latest fashionable playgrounds for the seemingly endless army of Americans abroad, but Romania, Slovakia, the Ukraine, Georgia and, of course, Russia are all economic disaster zones. Capitalism may be working in Seattle but it is most definitely not working in Bucharest.

The other factor drawing people here has of course been our much talked about economic boom. In the years 1996-2000 Ireland's Gross Domestic Product increased by 66%, after inflation is factored into account. For those of us who remember the 1980s, when unemployment hit 20% nationally and 70% in some parts of Galway city, it sometimes seems as if things as we knew them have vanished entirely. Like almost any country experiencing a boom,

Ireland is now awash with crap jobs. Many of us have been forced onto FÁS and VTOS schemes, in order to avoid the absolutely unthinkable: a job washing dishes at *Eddie Rocket's*. Property prices and rents have gone through the roof. And a cappuccino in the new Milano restaurant on Middle Street costs £1.65. It's the end of the world as we knew it. With our per capita national income now higher than Italy, France and the UK, we are suddenly just like any other 'rich' Western European country. In this context it's hardly surprising that we are now also experiencing our first significant trickle of immigration. And there will, of course, be much, much more: for every black person or sallow-skinned Eastern European you see in the street today, several more will arrive in the near future; because even the crappiest job here—yes, even *Eddie Rocket's*—is heaven compared to the possible alternatives in, say, Slovakia or Sierra Leone. The Minister for Justice can introduce all the harsh anti-immigration legislation he likes, but people will continue to come here. Immigration is now an inescapable fact of life in Ireland.

However, the reaction of some to our new-found neighbours has been a predictable and opportunistic attempt to stir things up. The *Sunday World* and *Sunday Independent* have both run lurid anti-immigrant 'stories', the worst of which appeared last year. Under the screaming headline "Refugee Maniac Covers Dublin Woman's Body With Vicious Bites", the *Sunday World* 'informed' us of an assault carried out by a Kosovar against his Irish wife. It was an absolutely clear-cut and appalling case of domestic violence, but had nothing whatsoever to do either with his nationality or his status as a refugee. Never mind the reality, just give us a headline and make it snappy! One of the results of this sort of 'journalism' has been a sharp increase in the number of Irish citizens willing to get up off their fat arses and go out and physically attack the foreign-looking people they see around them. It is only a matter of time before someone on some dark Irish street is knifed or battered to death. And when this happens the media whores sitting smugly in the offices of the *Sunday World* and *Sunday Independent* will be absolutely as guilty as the actual perpetrators.

Our politicians have, of course, been no better. Minister for Justice John O'Donoghue has talked endlessly about 'floods' of immigrants, while some of his party colleagues have gone in for even more exotic descriptions. During the 1997 General Election a number of Fianna Fáil candidates in Dublin, including recent jailbird Liam Lawlor, produced specifically anti-immigrant leaflets in their own constituencies. The worst of these came from Fianna Fáil councillor and candidate in Dublin South West, Colm McGrath. McGrath's leaflet claimed that if the "flood" wasn't stopped, the constituency would soon be "swamped" by refugees whose "way of life is entirely alien and includes, among other things, sacrificing animals during religious rituals". Since then Colm McGrath has departed from Fianna Fáil after refusing to co-operate with the party's internal inquiry into donations received by candidates. He was, it seems, too obvious a crook even for them.

The other predominant response has come from what might be described as the liberals—the Labour Party, the Greens and Sinn Féin. They have quite rightly been critical of the boot boy anti-immigrant language used by the Minister for Justice and others. And they have, to their credit, opposed some of his more repressive proposals such as 'flotels'. But the one thing liberals everywhere have in common is that they are all itching to get into government which, in this case, means hopping into bed with either Fianna Fáil or Fine Gael after the next General Election. It also means accepting the EU-wide 'Fortress Europe' anti-immigration policy on which the present government's policy is based. When I hear a spokesman for Labour, the Greens or Sinn Féin criticising John O'Donoghue's approach, I welcome it because it makes life easier for immigrants and cuts down slightly on the amount of xenophobic garbage I have to listen to; every little does help. But I am also acutely aware that a government containing Labour, the Greens or Sinn Féin—a definite possibility after the next election—would basically continue the present policy of trying to stop people coming into the country and deporting them when they manage to slip through the net. Whatever their rhetoric, the policies of these parties amount to little more than a wish to slip a velvet glove onto John O'Donoghue's iron fist.

In a world around which money is allowed to flow absolutely freely, it is completely reactionary to support any form of immigration controls. An Irish businessman such as Tony O'Reilly (owner of the *Sunday Independent, Irish Independent, Sunday Tribune, Evening Herald* and former chairman of Heinz) has the freedom to invest his money wherever he so chooses. O'Reilly's attitude is a good example of the way the ruling business class think about national boundaries. He is a US citizen and, as a result, pays no tax in Ireland. In 1988 he was chairman of Pennsylvania for Bush and was, at one stage, even tipped for possible inclusion in Bush senior's cabinet as Secretary for Trade. And he recently received a knighthood from Her Majesty Queen Elizabeth. The world is, almost literally, at his feet. While the likes of O'Reilly is free to profiteer in Asia, Eastern Europe, Africa and South America, how can it be morally defensible to support a policy which denies poverty-stricken individuals from those same parts of the world the right to live and work here, if they should so choose?

The woolly liberal answer to this question goes something like this: 'I absolutely sympathise with the tragic situation these people find themselves in, and we here in Ireland must do whatever we can to help them. But this does not mean an open door policy when it comes to immigration. This would simply lead to chaos and would in many ways make the situation much worse.' The problem with this sort of woolly liberal talk is that it tries to obscure the undeniable reality that, in the so-called 'Third World' and in Eastern Europe, chaos is already at hand. But, of course, the woolly liberal can live quite comfortably in a chaos-ridden world, as long as the chaos doesn't come anywhere near the end of the leafy lane where he typically lives. In such a world as this, it is not an anti-racist's job to make constructive suggestions as to how the Irish ruling elite might 'sort out' their immigration policy. As far as I'm concerned, anyone who wishes to come and live here, legally or otherwise, is welcome to do so. Who am I to stand in their way? And anyone who does try to stand in their way automatically becomes my enemy.

This has nothing to do with a sentimental attachment to the 'downtrodden of the world' or any such woolly liberal concept, but is, instead, a simple matter of solidarity. The same economic and political forces which have brought chaos to their lives are constantly trying to bring chaos to mine. We are all at the mercy of the US Federal Reserve and the European Central Bank. This country, this city does not in any meaningful sense 'belong' to the likes of me, but is owned lock, stock and barrel by the Tony O'Reillys, the Ben Dunnes and the ladies and gentlemen who sit on the Galway Chamber of Commerce. And when they pop their clogs, as even multi-millionaires must, they'll pass it all on to their pampered pasty-faced children. I can think of no earthly reason why I should wish to protect the borders of Ireland Incorporated from small groups of Nigerians and Romanians who have done me no harm whatsoever.

Of course the vast majority of people don't think like this at all. Most Irish people think that Bertie Ahern is a 'nice guy', whatever that means, and say 'fair play' to Denis O'Brien for making £230 million from ESAT Digifone. After all, most people think of Denis O'Brien as one of 'us' whereas a Romanian or a Nigerian is definitely thought of as one of 'them'. This very comforting, but entirely false view of the world is the glue which holds the system together. If the majority of Irish people were to suddenly come face to face with the reality of their own political and economic powerlessness, our millionaire class and the political parties they own might very quickly find themselves applying for asylum, in Vienna or Paris, like latter-day members of the Czar's extended family. Liberal calls for tolerance and multicultural evenings are well and good. But they are not enough, because racism is not caused, primarily, by cultural misunderstandings between members of different ethnic groups. Nor will it be defeated by preaching brotherly love in some fuzzy, almost Christian, sense.

Racism is the potentially deadly force that it is, precisely because it is a system of thinking whereby particular ethnic groups become lightning conductors for resentments—for example, about housing—which, in and of themselves, are entirely justified. In this sense it represents a dangerous new weapon in the ideological arsenal of the Irish ruling elite. And they are loving every minute of it. Every time someone from inner city Dublin phones *Liveline* to complain about refugees getting Corporation houses, the property speculators all light another cigar and have a good loud laugh. And when unemployment returns, as it undoubtedly one day will, the *Sunday Independent* will blame the Nigerians and Romanians for that too. The most urgent task at hand for anti-racists is to educate people to take their resentments out on the real enemy.

It is not enough to rant and rave in abstract about 'big business'. The enemy has to be unmasked, given a recognisable face. There is no shortage of possibilities. The crowd who come to Galway to live it up during the Oyster Festival and those who stay in the Great Southern Hotel during Race Week spring immediately to mind. Or if we could somehow manage to get Irish people forced to wait for a bus in the rain to picture Denis O'Brien's fat chauffer-driven face, rather than wasting their time resenting the black man who just drove past in a ten-year-old car, then we would be making real progress. And maybe then our new-found friends from Africa and Eastern Europe would find walking our streets just a little easier.

Red Banner magazine, June 2001

Kerry On My Mind

Kerry On My Mind: Of Poets, Pedagogues and Place is a collection of essays by Kerry poet/teacher Gabriel Fitzmaurice. This book combines literary and social criticism. In it Fitzmaurice sets out his ideas concerning the relationship between the writer and society. Articles on subjects such as the threat to life in rural Ireland fit snugly in with literary essays. For Fitzmaurice the literary is inextricably linked to the social. His roles as teacher and poet are interwoven. If it's art for art's sake you want, then he is definitely not your man. 'My Own Place' is important to the collection. It begins with a quotation from an early poem of his own

> Like a dog and its master
> Like a ship on the water,
> I need you, you bitch,
> Newtown.

but finishes with the observation, "I don't suppose I would write 'I need you, you bitch, Newtown' now. But the best love is based on giving, and I would give Moyvane anything I have to give." (Newtown was the name which the British imposed on Moyvane.) Place is important to Gabriel Fitzmaurice. He argues that much contemporary poetry suffers from belonging 'to no community'. There is an echo of Patrick Kavanagh's parochialism here. He talks of a 'Listowel school' of writers in which he situates John B Keane, Brendan Kennelly, and Bryan Mac Mahon. In essays on each of these he argues that they all give their depictions of the ordinary a touch of magic. He is by no means uncritical of his place. In 'Missing the Master' he recalls 'a thought police: the relentless and often brutal system of examining Christian Doctine'. He does, though, tend to let the backwoods men off the hook later in the same essay when he refers to the threat which teachers now face of being sued for implementing 'Stay Safe'. This threat did not fall to Kerry from outer space. It comes from a rump who are more a rural phenomenon than an urban one. He argues that poetry needs to return to music and notes the rise of American New Formalism as a development which might give it back its song. Whether you happen to agree with him or not you have to admit that Gabriel Fitzmaurice nails his colours firmly to the mast. *Kerry On My Mind* is well worth a read.

Galway Advertiser, June 10th, 1999

The literary magazine we really need

Literary magazines are a strange breed of publication. When I first began reading them around five years ago, they often seemed like documents sent from a parallel universe, full of aspiring poets, novels-in-progress and critics babbling on in a bizarre language all of their own. Of course this was part of their charm. They opened up a new world of glittering words and offered a possible means of escape from the drab reality of everyday things. For the most part, they had nothing to do with reality as such, seeming to exist on an altogether higher "aesthetic" level. It was just what I wanted! These were the places I would "become a writer". Or something like that. I had a poem accepted in a small magazine in England and it was as if I'd won the Nobel Prize. For a few weeks I was a pompous little literary git. The predictable deluge of rejections arrived as well. But every acceptance was filed away as concrete proof that I wasn't wasting my time. Literary magazines can sometimes seem ephemeral publications; who, apart from a tiny band of writers, bothers to read them? My experience illustrates the role they play in nurturing nervous new writers plagued by insecurity and egotism. After a while it's not enough simply to get published. You want to get in to the top magazines such as *The Shop, Poetry Ireland Review, Fortnight* or *Metre*—the poetic premier league. On one level, Irish literary magazines do a fairly good job. By and large they are not closed shops. You sometimes get the feeling that a particular poem was published because of the name of its author rather than the quality of the work. There is undoubtedly an amount of what George Orwell once described as "(literary) wire-pulling and back-stairs crawling". However, this is a vice which has existed since men and women first put pen to paper which we are unlikely to stamp out.

The real weakness in the current crop of Irish literary magazines is that they all tend to present us with a world of glittering words entirely separated from the things and actions from which all words ultimately come. It wasn't always so. In 1940, Sean Ó Faolain founded *The Bell* which, until its demise in 1954, was probably the most influential literary magazine ever to emerge from this country. It was vital to the careers of writers such as Patrick Kavanagh, Frank O'Connor, Mary Lavin and others. The key thing about the magazine was that it didn't simply publish the best poetry and fiction. It was also sometimes the only place where real debate occurred about major political and social issues. It campaigned against censorship, offered opinions about everything and opposed the prevailing Gaelic, Catholic isolationist ideology which then dominated both literature and society. The literary landscape may be different today, but *The Bell* is still useful as an example of the sort of magazine we need. Such a magazine could, for example, nurture a revival in the art of satire, which all but died during the smug 1990s. These days the world of Irish letters occasionally gives the impression of being full of bad liberals desperate to meet presidents and ambassadors. A Marxist would say that, given our economic boom, this is not at all surprising. But surely there must be a few of us out there who aren't afraid to ask the awkward questions, to be occasionally cranky, occasionally wrong? The backlash has to start somewhere.

Galway Advertiser, March 2001

BOOKS REVIEWED

Walter Macken—Dreams On Paper by ULTAN MACKEN. Mercier Press, 2009.

The Fitzpatrick Tapes—The rise and fall of one man, one bank and one country by TOM LYONS & BRIAN CAREY. Penguin Ireland, 2011.

Once Upon A Time In The West: The Corrib Gas Controversy by LORNA SIGGINS. Transworld Ireland, 2010.

Calling the Tune by MAUREEN GALLAGHER. Wordsonthestreet, 2008.

The Given Note: Traditional Music and Irish Poetry by SEÁN CROSSON. Cambridge Scholars Publishing, 2008.

AZALEA—Journal of Korean Literature & Culture (Volume One). The Korea Institute, Harvard University, 2007.

Cromwell's Head by JONATHAN FITZGIBBONS. The National Archives (UK), 2008,

American Skin by KEN BRUEN. Brandon Books, 2006.

The Boy in the Ring by DAVE LORDAN. Salmon Poetry, 2007.

poems from Guantánamo—The Detainees Speak edited by MARK FALKOFF. University of Iowa Press, 2008,

The Ledwidge Treasury—Selected Poems. New Island, 2007.

Neoconservatism: Why We Need It by DOUGLAS MURRAY. Encounter Books, 2006.

Straight Left—A Journey Into Politics by RUAIRÍ QUINN. Hodder Headline Ireland, 2005.

Director's Cut by David Solway. Porcupine's Quill, 2003.

Stasiland: Stories From Behind The Berlin Wall by Anna Funder. Granta Books, 2003.

GB84 by DAVID PEACE. Faber & Faber, 2004.

An Arid Season by MICHAEL D HIGGINS. New Island Books, 2004.

101 Poems Against War. Edited by MATHEW HOLLIS and PAUL KEEGAN. Faber and Faber, 2003.

100 Poets Against the War. Edited by TODD SWIFT. SALT Publishing, 2003.

Irish Writers Against War. Edited by CONOR KOSTICK and KATHERINE MOORE. O'Brien Press, 2003.

An Irishwoman's Diary by MAUREEN GALLAGHER. 2004.

Koba the Dread by MARTIN AMIS. Jonathan Cape, 2002.

In The Blue House by MEAGHAN DELAHUNT. Bloomsbury, 2001.

Unacknowledged Legislation: Writers in the public sphere by CHRISTOPHER HITCHENS. Verso, London, 2001.

Kerry On My Mind: Of Poets, Pedagogues and Place by Gabriel Fitzmaurice. Salmon, 1999.

The Condemned Apple: Selected Poetry by Visar Zhiti. Green Integer, 2004.

Arthur & George by Julian Barnes. Random House, 2005.

Nordkraft by Jakob Ejersbo. McArthur & Co., 2004.

KEVIN HIGGINS facilitates poetry workshops at Galway Arts Centre; teaches creative writing at Galway Technical Institute and on the Brothers of Charity Away With Words programme. He is also Writer-in-Residence at Merlin Park Hospital and the poetry critic of the Galway Advertiser. He was a founding co-editor of *The Burning Bush* literary magazine. His first collection of poems *The Boy With No Face* was published by Salmon in February 2005 and was short-listed for the 2006 Strong Award. His second collection, *Time Gentlemen, Please*, was published in March 2008 by Salmon. One of the poems from *Time Gentlemen, Please*, 'My Militant Tendency', featured in the *Forward Book of Poetry* 2009. His work also features in the anthology *Identity Parade – New British and Irish Poets* (Ed Roddy Lumsden, Bloodaxe, 2010). *Frightening New Furniture* is his third collection of poems and was published in 2010 by Salmon Poetry. Kevin has read his work at most of the major literary festivals in Ireland and at Arts Council and Culture Ireland supported poetry events in Kansas City, USA (2006), Los Angeles, USA (2007), London, UK (2007), New York, USA (2008), Athens, Greece (2008); St. Louis, USA (2008), Chicago, USA (2009), Denver, USA (2010), Washington D.C (2011), Huntington, West Virginia, USA (2011), Geelong, Australia (2011) & Canberra, Australia (2011). As part of his Culture Ireland supported trip to Chicago in February 2009 he participated in and took first place in a specially arranged poetry slam at the Chicago's Green Mill Bar and Lounge, the birthplace of slam poetry. Kevin's fourth collection of poetry, *The Ghost In The Lobby*, will be published by Salmon Poetry in 2013. Kevin is co-organiser of Over The Edge literary events.